Chinese Cooking

Jean Paré

companyscoming.com
visit our ↑ web-site

Front Cover

Back Cover

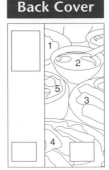

1. Yangtze Fried Rice, page 128
2. Wor Wonton Soup, page 48
3. Vegetarian Spring Rolls, page 22
4. Lemon Chicken, page 76
5. Steamed Pork Dumplings, page 38

Props Courtesy Of:
Kitchen Treasures

We gratefully acknowledge the following suppliers for their generous support of our Test Kitchen and Photo Studio:

Corelle ®
Lagostina ®
Tupperware ®

Chinese Cooking
Copyright © Company's Coming Publishing Limited
All rights reserved worldwide. No part of this book may be reproduced in any form by any means without written permission in advance from the publisher. Brief portions of this book may be reproduced for review purposes, provided credit is given to the source. Reviewers are invited to contact the publisher for additional information.

First Printing August 2003

National Library of Canada Cataloguing in Publication

Paré, Jean
    Chinese cooking / Jean Paré.

(Original series)
Includes index.
ISBN 1-896891-56-X

    1. Cookery, Chinese. I. Title. II. Series: Paré, Jean. Original series.

TX724.5.C5P37 2003   641.5951   C2003-901309-X

Published by
COMPANY'S COMING PUBLISHING LIMITED
2311 - 96 Street
Edmonton, Alberta, Canada T6N 1G3
Tel: (780) 450-6223   Fax: (780) 450-1857
www.companyscoming.com

Company's Coming is a registered trademark owned by Company's Coming Publishing Limited

Printed in Canada

Visit us on-line

companyscoming.com

Who We Are | Browse Cookbooks | Cooking Tonight? | Home

everyday ingredients

feature recipes

feature recipes — Cooking tonight? Check out this month's **feature recipes** absolutely FREE!

tips and tricks — Looking for some great kitchen helpers? **tips and tricks** are here to save the day!

reader circle — In search of answers to cooking or household questions? Do you have answers you'd like to share? Join the fun with **reader circle**, our on-line question and answer bulletin board. Great for swapping recipes too!

cooking links — Other interesting and informative web-sites are just a click away with **cooking links.**

cookbook search — Find cookbooks by title, description or food category using **cookbook search**.

contact us — We want to hear from you—**contact us** lets you offer suggestions for upcoming titles, or share your favourite recipes.

Company's Coming
COOKBOOKS

Canada's
**most popular
cookbooks!**

Company's Coming Cookbook Series

Quick & easy recipes, everyday ingredients!

Original Series

- Softcover, 160 pages
- 6" x 9" (15 cm x 23 cm) format
- Lay-flat binding
- Full colour photos
- Nutrition information

Greatest Hits Series

- Softcover, 106 & 124 pages
- 8" x 9 9/16" (20 cm x 24 cm) format
- Paperback binding
- Full colour photos
- Nutrition information

Lifestyle Series

- Softcover, 160 pages
- 8" x 10" (20 cm x 25 cm) format
- Paperback & spiral binding
- Full colour photos
- Nutrition information

Special Occasion Series

- Hardcover & softcover, 192 pages
- 8 1/2" x 11" (22 cm x 28 cm) format
- Durable sewn binding
- Full colour throughout
- Nutrition information

See page 157
for a complete listing
of __all__ cookbooks
or visit
companyscoming.com

Table of Contents

Glossary

Chopsticks

Soups

Noodles & Rice

Desserts

Recipe Index

What's New!

The Company's Coming Story . . .   6

Foreword.   7

Glossary   8

Chopsticks. 10

Appetizers 12

Dim Sum. 28

Soups 44

Main Dishes. 56

Noodles & Rice 118

Vegetable Dishes 132

Desserts. 141

Measurement Tables 150

Tip Index. 151

Recipe Index 151

Mail Order Form 158

What's New! 159

Cookbook Checklist. 160

The Company's Coming Story

Jean Paré grew up understanding that the combination of family, friends and home cooking is the essence of a good life. From her mother she learned to appreciate good cooking, while her father praised even her earliest attempts. When she left home she took with her many acquired family recipes, a love of cooking and an intriguing desire to read recipe books like novels!

"never share a recipe you wouldn't use yourself"

In 1963, when her four children had all reached school age, Jean volunteered to cater the 50th anniversary of the Vermilion School of Agriculture, now Lakeland College. Working out of her home, Jean prepared a dinner for over 1000 people which launched a flourishing catering operation that continued for over eighteen years. During that time she was provided with countless opportunities to test new ideas with immediate feedback—resulting in empty plates and contented customers! Whether preparing cocktail sandwiches for a house party or serving a hot meal for 1500 people, Jean Paré earned a reputation for good food, courteous service and reasonable prices.

"Why don't you write a cookbook?" Time and again, as requests for her recipes mounted, Jean was asked that question. Jean's response was to team up with her son, Grant Lovig, in the fall of 1980 to form Company's Coming Publishing Limited. April 14, 1981 marked the debut of "150 DELICIOUS SQUARES", the first Company's Coming cookbook in what soon would become Canada's most popular cookbook series.

Jean Paré's operation has grown steadily from the early days of working out of a spare bedroom in her home. Full-time staff includes marketing personnel located in major cities across Canada. Home Office is based in Edmonton, Alberta in a modern building constructed specially for the company.

Today the company distributes throughout Canada and the United States in addition to numerous overseas markets, all under the guidance of Jean's daughter, Gail Lovig. Best-sellers many times over in English, Company's Coming cookbooks have also been published in French and Spanish. Familiar and trusted in home kitchens around the world, Company's Coming cookbooks are offered in a variety of formats, including the original softcover series.

Jean Paré's approach to cooking has always called for quick and easy recipes using everyday ingredients. Even when travelling, she is constantly on the lookout for new ideas to share with her readers. At home, she can usually be found researching and writing recipes, or working in the company's test kitchen. Jean continues to gain new supporters by adhering to what she calls "the golden rule of cooking": never share a recipe you wouldn't use yourself. It's an approach that works—*millions of times over!*

Foreword

Chinese cuisine has made a great contribution to the world of food. The enduring popularity of Chinese food has a lot to do with the creative variety of fresh ingredients that are used. Meats, rice, noodles, vegetables and seasonings combine in so many ways to create dishes ranging in taste from subtle to spicy to screaming hot! Careful attention is paid to appearance, flavour, texture and fragrance, making Chinese dining a satisfying adventure for your senses!

Although North Americans often refer to Chinese cuisine as one unified cooking style, it can actually be separated into at least five main regions, all featuring distinct flavours and unique ingredients. Cantonese (southern) cuisine is famous for fried rice, roasted and grilled meats, and dim sum; Fukien (eastern) cuisine for soups and seafood; Peking (northern) cuisine for noodles, duck and the subtle use of seasonings; Honan (central) cuisine for sweet and sour food; and Szechuan (western) cuisine for hot and spicy dishes. In *Chinese Cooking*, you will find recipes that have been influenced by all of these regional cooking styles.

Interestingly, many of the dishes we associate with Chinese cuisine are really adaptations of traditional recipes or more recent inventions designed to accommodate the western palate. Familiar items such as chop suey and fortune cookies were actually created in the United States!

Chinese Cooking includes recipes for your favourite Chinese dishes and for new, exciting ones that you haven't tried yet. Take pleasure in the adventure of discovering new flavours. Familiarize yourself with the Asian section of your grocery store or local Asian market and if you come across ingredients that you don't know, refer to the Glossary on pages 8, 9 and 10 for more information.

When planning your meal, remember that Chinese cuisine centres around the concept of balance. The ideal Chinese meal strikes a balance between two categories: *cai*—meat and vegetable dishes, and the more basic *fan*—rice or other grain-based dishes. There must also be a balance between the more bland *yin* selections—often boiled or steamed, and the spicier, more heavily seasoned *yang* selections—often stir-fried, roasted or deep-fried. To make your meals even more authentic, use chopsticks!

Jean Paré

Each recipe has been analyzed using the most up-to-date version of the Canadian Nutrient File from Health Canada, which is based on the United States Department of Agriculture (USDA) Nutrient Data Base. If more than one ingredient is listed (such as "hard margarine or butter"), the first ingredient is used in the analysis. Where an ingredient reads "sprinkle," "optional," or "for garnish," it is not included as part of the nutrition information.

Margaret Ng, B.Sc. (Hon.), M.A.
Registered Dietitian

Glossary

Bamboo shoots: Ivory coloured, tender-crisp shoots add a nice crunch and distinct flavour to dishes. For ease and availability, use canned bamboo shoots. Found in Asian section of grocery stores.

Bean curd sheets (also called bean curd skin): Thin sheets made from soybean milk. The sheets are plastic-like and malleable, therefore used to wrap food for dim sums. May also be thinly sliced and added to stir-fry dishes. Found in frozen section of Asian grocery stores.

Bean sprouts (also called mung bean sprouts): A vegetable that adds subtle flavour and crunch to many different dishes. To retain crispness, do not overcook. Refrigerate airtight in plastic bag for only 2 to 3 days. Found in produce section of grocery stores.

Black bean sauce: There are two very different products available with the same name. The concentrated sauce is thick, somewhat chunky and paste-like. It should be used in small amounts since it has a strong flavour. What we refer to in our recipes as black bean sauce is thinner and smoother than the concentrated sauce. It can be used as is from the bottle. Found in Asian section of grocery stores.

Chili paste (also called sambal oelek, pronounced SAHM-bahl OH-lehk): This condiment for rice and curries is a mixture of chilies, brown sugar and salt. Found in Asian section of grocery stores.

Chinese sausage: A hard, dry sausage with a smoked, slightly sweet taste. It has a high fat content. Found in Asian grocery stores.

Chinese barbecue sauce: A unique flavour much different than the barbecue sauce we are all used to. A dark brown grainy paste that consists of ground dried fish, chili peppers, garlic, dried shrimp, ground peanuts, coriander seeds, star anise and Szechuan peppercorns. Found in Asian section of some large grocery stores and in Asian grocery stores.

Chinese chili sauce: A blend of chilies, garlic, vinegar, salt and sugar. Used as a condiment as well as added to stir-fries. Found in Asian section of grocery stores.

Chinese five-spice powder: A traditional Chinese blend of at least 5 spices (usually equal parts of star anise, fennel, cloves, cinnamon and Szechuan peppercorns). A very pungent spice, therefore use sparingly. Found in spice section of grocery stores.

Chinese satay sauce: A thick, grainy, paste-like sauce that is deep orange in colour (not to be confused with Chinese barbecue sauce). It is a concentrated sauce (not a dipping sauce) that consists of coconut extract, peanuts, onions, sugar, oil, tamarind and spices. Found in Asian section of some large grocery stores and in Asian grocery stores.

Cilantro (also called Chinese parsley): A fresh, distinct flavour and aroma that lends itself nicely to spicy foods. Available all year round. Found in produce section of grocery stores.

Gingerroot: The gnarled, knobby root of the ginger plant. A peppery and slightly sweet taste with a pungent and spicy aroma. The outer layer is peeled and the inner portion either finely grated or sliced and minced. In most cases the dry ground form is not a substitute because the flavour is very different. Refrigerate unused gingerroot tightly wrapped for up to 3 weeks or in freezer for up to 6 months. Found in bulk in the produce section or in bags in spice section of grocery stores.

Glutinous rice (also called sweet rice or sticky rice): Becomes sticky when cooked and is sweeter than regular rice. Commonly used in desserts and as a stuffing or coating in a variety of dim sums. Found in Asian section of some large grocery stores and in Asian grocery stores.

Glutinous rice flour (also called sweet rice flour): Made from glutinous rice (see above). This flour is responsible for the desired stickiness and chewiness of Asian pastries. Found in Asian section of

some large grocery stores and in Asian grocery stores.

Hoisin (HOY-sihn) sauce (also called Peking sauce): Sweet and spicy mixture of soybeans, garlic, chili peppers and spices. Mainly used as a condiment and to flavour meat, poultry and shellfish dishes. Found in Asian section of grocery stores.

Lotus seed paste: Lotus seeds are made into a sweetened light brown paste and used for pastries and dim sum specialties. Found in Asian grocery stores.

Lychee (LEE-chee): The flavour of this fruit is sweet. Lychees are juicy and smooth. We used canned lychees, which are an acceptable substitute when fresh lychees are not in season. Found in Asian section of grocery stores.

Oyster sauce: Thick dark brown sauce made from oysters, brine and soy sauce. Mainly used in stir-fries and as a condiment. Found in Asian section of grocery stores and where soy sauce and other condiments are found.

Peanut oil: This oil is particularly good for use in frying because of its high smoke point. The distinctive peanut flavour also makes this oil a good choice in salad dressings and stir-fries. Chinese peanut oils have a more distinct peanut flavour than North American peanut oils. Found where all cooking oils are located in grocery stores.

Sesame oil: There are light (or golden) and dark varieties of this oil. For a richer flavour, look for the darker kind, which has a dark amber colour and a nutty flavour. It is generally added in small quantities as a flavour accent. Found where all cooking oils are located in grocery stores. (Note: Sesame oil can be omitted if preferred but will affect the flavour of the dish.)

Straw mushrooms: Delicate-flavoured small mushrooms (1 to 1 1/2 inches, 2.5 to 3.8 cm, in diameter) grown on beds of straw. Also called paddy straw mushrooms or grass mushrooms. Available in a can or plastic package and found in Asian grocery stores. Small fresh white mushrooms can be used as a substitute.

Sweet red bean paste: A sweetened paste made from dried beans. A popular filling for steamed buns and pastries. Found in Asian section of grocery stores.

Tofu (also called bean curd or soybean curd): A bland, slightly nutty flavour that takes on the flavour of food that it is cooked with. Most commonly sold in cakes (soft, medium, firm and extra firm). Refrigerate for up to one week. Store covered with water and replace water daily. Found in grocery stores, health-food stores and in Asian grocery stores.

Wheat starch (also called non-glutinous flour): Used to make the thin, translucent casing for popular shrimp-stuffed pastries (har gow). Is sometimes used to thicken sauce. Found in Asian section of some large grocery stores and in Asian grocery stores.

Chopsticks

Chinese for "quick little one" or "something fast." Chopsticks are made from a variety of materials—ivory, silver, lacquer and specialty woods. Everyday chopsticks are mostly made from bamboo. They range in length from 10 inches (25 cm) to over 18 inches (45 cm). The longer chopsticks are used as a cooking utensil for stirring, whipping and tasting, and are made from bamboo as it won't conduct heat. Although chopsticks are very common in both the Chinese and Japanese cultures, Chinese chopsticks are squared and more blunt at the narrow end while Japanese chopsticks are rounder and more pointed at the end.

Glossary

How to Use Chopsticks

1. Place upper portion of 1 chopstick in curve between thumb and first finger (index finger) of "eating" hand, resting lower portion against side of fourth (ring) finger in a stationary position. You should not be able to wiggle this chopstick.

2. Place upper portion of second chopstick above first chopstick, between tip of thumb and side of first finger and resting against middle finger (similar to how you might hold a pen or pencil). You should be able to wiggle this chopstick.

3. By moving your index finger, move the top chopstick up and down, creating an "open" and "close" action against the bottom chopstick, perfect for picking up everything from dim sum dumplings to pea pods.

Chopstick Etiquette

Yes, just as with knives and forks, there are manners when using chopsticks. We're not sure how authentic these points of etiquette are. However, they might keep you from offending your host.

1. To prevent "double dipping," use larger ends of chopsticks to choose food from a common platter. The trick here is to remember to turn them around before starting to eat again!

2. Don't pass food from one pair of chopsticks to another.

3. Don't stick chopsticks upright in rice.

4. Don't spear food with chopsticks. If food needs to be "cut," pick up food and bite off portion.

5. Use chopsticks to eat solid pieces in soup (such as wonton, broccoli, pea pods), then use the open-bowled spoon for the broth.

6. Don't use chopsticks to pull bowls or plates towards you.

Chopsticks

Green Onion Cakes

Green onion and sesame oil are the predominant flavours in these chewy pancakes. Serve with Sweet And Sour Sauce, page 15, Plum Sauce, page 23, sour cream or chili paste.

All-purpose flour	2 1/2 cups	625 mL
Wheat starch (see Note)	1/2 cup	125 mL
Granulated sugar	1 tsp.	5 mL
Salt	1 tsp.	5 mL
Very hot water, approximately	1 cup	250 mL
Sesame oil	1 1/2 tbsp.	25 mL
Thinly sliced green onion	1 1/2 cups	375 mL
Cooking oil	1/4 cup	60 mL

Combine flour, wheat starch, sugar and salt in large bowl.

Slowly stir in enough hot water until ball starts to form. Knead on lightly floured surface until smooth and elastic. Wrap in plastic wrap. Let rest for 30 minutes. Divide into 12 portions. Keep dough covered in plastic wrap to prevent drying out.

Shape 1 portion into flattened disc. Roll out very thinly to 6 inch (15 cm) circle on lightly greased surface with rolling pin that has been greased with sesame oil.

Sprinkle with about 2 tbsp. (30 mL) green onion. Roll up tightly, jelly roll-style. Pinch edge and ends together to seal. Roll and pull to shape into 9 inch (22 cm) log. Twist several times in 1 direction. Shape into tight coil on lightly greased surface. Roll out to about 4 1/2 inch (11 cm) circle with lightly greased rolling pin. Repeat with remaining dough and green onion.

Heat 1 tbsp. (15 mL) cooking oil in large frying pan on medium until hot. Cook, 3 at a time, for about 2 minutes per side, flattening with lifter occasionally, until brown patches appear on both sides. Do not overcook. They should be soft, pliable and chewy inside but crisp on outside. Remove to paper towels to drain. Repeat, adding cooking oil to pan each time, until all cakes are cooked. Serve warm. Makes 12 cakes.

1 cake: 184 Calories; 6.9 g Total Fat (3.6 g Mono, 2.3 g Poly, 0.6 g Sat); 0 mg Cholesterol; 27 g Carbohydrate; 1 g Fibre; 4 g Protein; 201 mg Sodium

(continued on next page)

Pictured on front cover.

Note: All-purpose flour may be substituted for wheat starch. However, wheat starch does make green onion cakes more chewy without being doughy.

Battered Dry Ribs

*These salty and slightly sweet golden brown ribs are
the perfect finger food. Delicious!*

Sweet and sour cut pork ribs, cut into 1-bone portions	3 lbs.	1.4 kg
Water, to cover		
Hoisin sauce	3 tbsp.	50 mL
Apple cider vinegar	2 tbsp.	30 mL
Brown sugar, packed	2 tbsp.	30 mL
Water	2 tbsp.	30 mL
Garlic clove, minced (or 1/4 tsp., 1 mL, powder)	1	1
Salt	2 tsp.	10 mL
All-purpose flour	1/3 cup	75 mL
Large eggs	4	4

Cooking oil, for deep-frying

Boil ribs in first amount of water in large pot or Dutch oven for 20 minutes. Drain. Cool. Blot dry.

Combine next 6 ingredients in large bowl. Stir.

Add flour. Mix. Add eggs, 1 at a time, stirring well with whisk after each addition, until batter is smooth. Add ribs. Stir until coated.

Deep-fry, in 2 or 3 batches, in hot (375°F, 190°C) cooking oil for about 2 minutes, stirring often, until browned. Remove to paper towels to drain. Makes about 100 ribs.

6 ribs: 312 Calories; 26 g Total Fat (13.3 g Mono, 5.3 g Poly, 5.5 g Sat); 94 mg Cholesterol; 6 g Carbohydrate; trace Fibre; 13 g Protein; 417 mg Sodium

Appetizers **13**

Deep-Fried Wontons

*These crispy wontons are filled with well-seasoned pork
and shrimp. Serve them with Sweet And Sour Sauce, page 15, or Plum Sauce,
page 23, or add these to a soup of your choice—just skip the deep-frying
and cook in boiling water instead.*

Lean ground pork	1/2 lb.	225 g
Raw shrimp, peeled and deveined, finely chopped	1/4 lb.	113 g
Dry sherry	1 tbsp.	15 mL
Soy sauce	2 tsp.	10 mL
Cornstarch	1 tsp.	5 mL
Salt	1/2 tsp.	2 mL
Pepper	1/8 tsp.	0.5 mL
Garlic powder	1/8 tsp.	0.5 mL
Ground ginger	1/8 tsp.	0.5 mL
Cold water	2 tbsp.	30 mL
Cornstarch	1 tbsp.	15 mL
Wonton wrappers	84	84

Cooking oil, for deep-frying

Mix first 9 ingredients in medium bowl.

Stir water into cornstarch in small dish. Set aside.

1. Lay 1 wrapper on work surface with 1 corner closest to you. Keep unused wrappers covered with damp tea towel to prevent drying out. Place 1/2 tsp. (2 mL) filling in centre of wrapper. Brush adjacent edges of wrapper with cornstarch paste. 2. Fold up 1 corner to meet opposite corner, forming triangle. Press edges together very firmly to seal. Brush opposite corners with cornstarch paste. 3. Bring opposite corners together under filling. Press together firmly. Repeat with remaining filling and wrappers, keeping filled wontons covered with damp tea towels.

(continued on next page)

Deep-fry, a few at a time, in hot (375°F, 190°C) cooking oil until crisp and golden brown. Remove to paper towels to drain. Makes about 84 wontons.

1 wonton: 50 Calories; 2.6 g Total Fat (1.5 g Mono, 0.8 g Poly, 0.2 g Sat); 4 mg Cholesterol; 5 g Carbohydrate; 0 g Fibre; 2 g Protein; 72 mg Sodium

Pictured on page 17.

To Make Ahead: Freeze uncooked wontons in single layer on waxed paper-lined baking sheets until firm. Transfer to airtight container. Store in freezer for up to 2 months. Wontons can be deep-fried frozen.

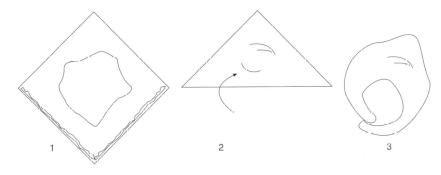

Sweet And Sour Sauce

A glossy, moderately thick sauce with a great combination of flavours.

Water	3/4 cup	175 mL
Cornstarch	1 1/2 tbsp.	25 mL
White vinegar	1/3 cup	75 mL
Granulated sugar	1/3 cup	75 mL
Ketchup	2 tbsp.	30 mL
Soy sauce	1 1/2 tsp.	7 mL

Stir water into cornstarch in small saucepan. Heat and stir on medium until boiling and thickened. Remove from heat.

Add remaining 4 ingredients. Stir until sugar is dissolved. Makes 1 1/3 cups (325 mL).

2 tbsp. (30 mL): 33 Calories; trace Total Fat (0 g Mono, 0 g Poly, 0 g Sat); 0 mg Cholesterol; 9 g Carbohydrate; trace Fibre; trace Protein; 80 mg Sodium

Pictured on page 72.

Salty Chinese Almonds

These attractive, glossy almonds are sweet and
salty with a mild, lingering heat in the aftertaste. The wonderful
combination of flavours is sure to stimulate your appetite.

Soy sauce	3 tbsp.	50 mL
Brown sugar, packed	2 tsp.	10 mL
Ground ginger	1/8 tsp.	0.5 mL
Garlic powder	1/8 tsp.	0.5 mL
Cayenne pepper	1/8 tsp.	0.5 mL
Whole almonds, toasted (see Tip, page 103)	1 cup	250 mL
Cooking oil	1 tsp.	5 mL

Combine first 5 ingredients in small saucepan.

Add almonds. Bring to a boil on medium-high. Boil for about 5 minutes, stirring often, until liquid is absorbed.

Drizzle cooking oil over almonds. Stir well. Spread out on ungreased baking sheet. Bake in 250°F (120°C) oven for about 10 minutes, stirring twice, until almonds are slightly dry. Makes 1 cup (250 mL).

1/4 cup (60 mL): 249 Calories; 20.8 g Total Fat (13.4 g Mono, 4.5 g Poly, 1.9 g Sat);
0 mg Cholesterol; 11 g Carbohydrate; 2 g Fibre; 9 g Protein; 788 mg Sodium

Pictured on page 17.

1. Sang Choy Bow, page 20
2. Hot Mustard Sauce, page 27
3. Salty Chinese Almonds, above
4. Deep-Fried Wontons, page 14
5. Shrimp Toast, page 19
6. Ham And Chicken Rolls, page 26

Props Courtesy Of: Cherison Enterprises Inc.

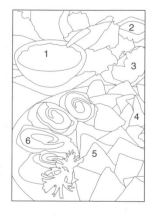

Appetizers

Shrimp Toast

These golden, triangular appetizers taste great warm or at room temperature. These freeze well and can easily be reheated in the oven for a quick, crispy treat.

Egg white (large), fork-beaten	1	1
Finely chopped raw shrimp, blotted dry	1/2 cup	125 mL
Finely chopped water chestnuts	2 tbsp.	30 mL
Green onion, finely chopped	1	1
Cornstarch	2 tsp.	10 mL
Dry sherry	2 tsp.	10 mL
Salt	1/2 tsp.	2 mL
Bread slices, crusts removed	7	7
Cooking oil, for deep-frying		

Put first 7 ingredients into blender or food processor. Process with on/off motion several times, scraping down sides, until paste-like consistency.

Spread about 2 tbsp. (30 mL) shrimp mixture on each bread slice. Cut each slice diagonally into 4 triangles.

Deep-fry, several triangles at a time, shrimp-side down, in hot (375°F, 190°C) cooking oil for about 2 minutes, turning once, until crisp and golden. Remove to paper towels to drain. Makes 28 triangles.

1 triangle: 44 Calories; 2.6 g Total Fat (1.5 g Mono, 0.7 g Poly, 0.2 g Sat); 4 mg Cholesterol; 4 g Carbohydrate; trace Fibre; 1 g Protein; 79 mg Sodium

Pictured on page 17.

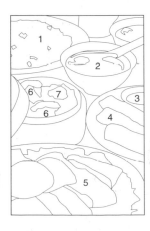

1. Yangtze Fried Rice, page 128
2. Wor Wonton Soup, page 48
3. Plum Sauce, page 23
4. Vegetarian Spring Rolls, page 22
5. Lemon Chicken, page 76
6. Shrimp Tail Purses, page 32
7. Steamed Pork Dumplings, page 38

Props Courtesy Of: Kitchen Treasures

Sang Choy Bow

Crisp lettuce leaves with a delicious crab and pork filling.

FILLING

Chinese dried mushrooms	4	4
Boiling water, to cover		
Water	1 tsp.	5 mL
Cornstarch	1 tsp.	5 mL
Peanut (or cooking) oil	1 tbsp.	15 mL
Garlic cloves, minced (or 1/2 tsp., 2 mL, powder)	2	2
Finely grated peeled gingerroot	1/2 tsp.	2 mL
Chopped green onion	1/4 cup	60 mL
Ground pork	6 oz.	170 g
Can of crabmeat, drained and cartilage removed, flaked	4 1/4 oz.	120 g
Chopped water chestnuts	1/4 cup	60 mL
Oyster sauce	2 tbsp.	30 mL
Soy sauce	1 tbsp.	15 mL
Dry sherry	1 tbsp.	15 mL
Sesame oil	1 tsp.	5 mL
Iceberg lettuce leaves	12	12

Filling: Put mushrooms into small bowl. Add boiling water. Let stand for 20 minutes until softened. Drain. Remove and discard stems. Chop caps finely. Set aside.

Stir water into cornstarch in small cup. Set aside.

Heat peanut oil in wok or large frying pan on high. Add garlic, ginger and green onion. Stir-fry for about 1 minute until fragrant.

Add ground pork. Stir-fry for 3 to 5 minutes until no longer pink.

Add next 6 ingredients. Stir-fry until combined. Stir cornstarch mixture. Stir into pork mixture for about 3 minutes until thickened. Add mushrooms. Heat and stir until hot. Makes about 1 1/2 cups (375 mL) filling.

(continued on next page)

Appetizers

Spoon 2 tbsp. (30 mL) filling on each lettuce leaf. Roll up to eat. Makes 12 appetizers.

1 appetizer: 73 Calories; 4.7 g Total Fat (2 g Mono, 0.8 g Poly, 1.4 g Sat); 10 mg Cholesterol; 3 g Carbohydrate; trace Fibre; 4 g Protein; 410 mg Sodium

Pictured on page 17.

Princess Shrimp Rolls

These crunchy, golden brown rolls are bursting with flavour. Serve with Sweet And Sour Sauce, page 15, Plum Sauce, page 23, or soy sauce.

Raw shrimp, peeled and deveined	10 oz.	285 g
Fresh pea pods, finely shredded	6	6
Finely chopped green onion	1	1
Cornstarch	2 tsp.	10 mL
Finely grated peeled gingerroot	1/2 tsp.	2 mL
Salt	1/2 tsp.	2 mL
All-purpose flour	2 tbsp.	30 mL
Water	2 tbsp.	30 mL
Spring roll wrappers (6 inch, 15 cm, square)	8	8
Cooking oil, for deep-frying		

Chop shrimp into pea-size pieces.

Combine next 5 ingredients in small bowl. Add shrimp. Stir.

Combine flour and water in small cup until smooth.

Lay 1 wrapper on work surface with 1 corner closest to you. Keep unused wrappers covered with damp tea towel to prevent drying out. Place 2 tbsp. (30 mL) filling in centre of wrapper in oblong shape. Brush edges of wrapper with flour paste. Fold up 1 corner over filling. Fold in both sides. Roll up tightly to seal. Repeat with remaining filling and wrappers, keeping filled rolls covered with damp tea towel.

Deep-fry in hot (375°F, 190°C) cooking oil for about 3 minutes, turning once, until crisp and golden. Remove to paper towels to drain. Makes 8 shrimp rolls.

1 shrimp roll: 174 Calories; 5.6 g Total Fat (2.9 g Mono, 1.8 g Poly, 0.5 g Sat); 44 mg Cholesterol; 21 g Carbohydrate; trace Fibre; 9 g Protein; 371 mg Sodium

Pictured on page 72.

Vegetarian Spring Rolls

Your guests will devour these crispy rolls. Serve with
Sweet And Sour Sauce, page 15, or Plum Sauce, page 23.

Oyster sauce	2 tbsp.	30 mL
Cold water	1 tbsp.	15 mL
Dry sherry	2 tsp.	10 mL
Sesame oil	2 tsp.	10 mL
Cornstarch	2 tsp.	10 mL
Garlic salt	1/4 tsp.	1 mL
Ground ginger	1/4 tsp.	1 mL
Salt	1/4 tsp.	1 mL
FILLING		
Chinese dried mushrooms	6	6
Boiling water, to cover		
Bean threads (or rice vermicelli)	3 oz.	85 g
Boiling water, to cover		
Cooking oil	1 tbsp.	15 mL
Shredded fresh spinach, lightly packed	1 cup	250 mL
Grated carrot	1/3 cup	75 mL
Thinly sliced green onion	1/3 cup	75 mL
Finely chopped canned bamboo shoots	2 tbsp.	30 mL
Finely chopped water chestnuts	2 tbsp.	30 mL
All-purpose flour	2 tbsp.	30 mL
Water	2 tbsp.	30 mL
Spring roll wrappers (6 inch, 15 cm, square)	20	20
Cooking oil, for deep-frying		
Roasted salted peanuts, ground to fine crumbs (optional)	1 tbsp.	15 mL

Stir first 8 ingredients in small dish until smooth. Set aside.

Filling: Put mushrooms into small bowl. Add boiling water. Let stand for 20 minutes until softened. Drain. Remove and discard stems. Slice caps thinly. Set aside.

(continued on next page)

Break bean threads into large bowl. Add boiling water. Let stand for 2 minutes. Drain well. Return threads to bowl.

Heat wok or large frying pan on medium-high until very hot. Add first amount of cooking oil. Add next 5 ingredients. Add mushrooms. Stir-fry for about 2 minutes until carrot is soft and liquid from spinach is evaporated. Stir oyster sauce mixture. Stir into spinach mixture until boiling and thickened. Turn out onto large plate to cool for 10 minutes. Combine with bean threads. Toss together. Makes 2 2/3 cups (650 mL) filling.

Stir flour and water in small cup until smooth.

Lay 1 wrapper on work surface with 1 corner closest to you. Keep unused wrappers covered with damp tea towel to prevent drying out. Brush edges of wrapper with flour paste. Place generous 2 tbsp. (30 mL) filling in centre of wrapper. Fold up 1 corner over filling. Fold in both sides. Roll up tightly to seal. Repeat with remaining filling and wrappers, keeping filled rolls covered with damp tea towel.

Deep-fry in hot (375°F, 190°C) cooking oil for about 2 minutes, turning once, until crisp and golden. Remove to paper towels to drain.

Sprinkle with peanuts while still warm. Makes 20 spring rolls.

1 spring roll: 171 Calories; 6.3 g Total Fat (3.4 g Mono, 2 g Poly, 0.5 g Sat); 3 mg Cholesterol; 25 g Carbohydrate; trace Fibre; 4 g Protein; 381 mg Sodium

Pictured on page 18 and on back cover.

Plum Sauce

A rich, thick sauce with a sweet taste. Serve with just about anything!

Plum jam	1 cup	250 mL
Apricot jam	2 tbsp.	30 mL
White vinegar	2 tbsp.	30 mL
Granulated sugar	2 tsp.	10 mL
Ground ginger	1/8 tsp.	0.5 mL

Measure all 5 ingredients into small bowl. Stir until sugar is dissolved. Makes about 1 cup (250 mL).

2 tbsp. (30 mL): 114 Calories; 0.1 g Total Fat (0.1 g Mono, 0 g Poly, trace Sat); 0 mg Cholesterol; 30 g Carbohydrate; trace Fibre; trace Protein; 18 mg Sodium

Pictured on page 18.

Egg Rolls

These large, tightly rolled appetizers have a crispy exterior and
a soft, fresh-tasting filling. The many contrasting flavours combine very well.
Serve with Sweet And Sour Sauce, page 15, or Plum Sauce, page 23.

Chinese dried mushrooms	3	3
Boiling water, to cover		
Cooking oil	1 tbsp.	15 mL
Lean ground pork	1/2 lb.	225 g
Garlic clove, minced (or 1/4 tsp., 1 mL, powder)	1	1
Raw shrimp, peeled and deveined, chopped	1/2 lb.	225 g
Shredded bok choy	2 cups	500 mL
Fresh bean sprouts, chopped once or twice	1 cup	250 mL
Can of water chestnuts, drained, minced	8 oz.	227 mL
Green onions, chopped	5	5
Soy sauce	4 tsp.	20 mL
Dry sherry	1 tbsp.	15 mL
Granulated sugar	1 tsp.	5 mL
Salt	1 tsp.	5 mL
All-purpose flour	2 tbsp.	30 mL
Water	2 tbsp.	30 mL
Egg roll wrappers	12	12

Cooking oil, for deep-frying

Put mushrooms into small bowl. Add boiling water. Let stand for 20 minutes until softened. Drain. Remove and discard stems. Chop caps finely. Set aside.

Heat first amount of cooking oil in wok or large frying pan on medium-high. Add ground pork and garlic. Stir-fry for about 1 minute until no pink remains in pork.

Add mushrooms and next 4 ingredients. Stir-fry for 3 minutes.

Add next 5 ingredients. Stir-fry for about 4 minutes until liquid is evaporated. Cool.

(continued on next page)

Stir flour and water in small dish until smooth paste.

Lay 1 wrapper on work surface with 1 corner closest to you. Keep unused wrappers covered with damp tea towel to prevent drying out. Place 5 tbsp. (75 mL) filling in centre of wrapper in oblong shape. Brush edges of wrapper with flour paste. Fold up 1 corner over filling. Fold in both sides. Roll up tightly to seal. Repeat with remaining filling and wrappers, keeping filled rolls covered with damp tea towel.

Deep-fry, 2 at a time, seam-side down, in hot (375°F, 190°C) cooking oil for about 2 minutes, turning once, until crisp and golden. Remove to paper towels to drain. Makes 12 egg rolls.

1 egg roll: 233 Calories; 10.5 g Total Fat (5.3 g Mono, 2.4 g Poly, 2 g Sat); 38 mg Cholesterol; 24 g Carbohydrate; 1 g Fibre; 10 g Protein; 538 mg Sodium

To Make Ahead: Freeze prepared egg rolls in airtight container. Arrange frozen egg rolls on ungreased baking sheet. Heat in 350°F (175°C) oven for about 10 minutes until soft.

Shrimp Crackers

Serve with appetizers or as part of a main meal. These are crunchy and crisp with a delicate shrimp flavour.

Uncooked shrimp crackers (see Note)	1/4 cup	60 mL
Cooking oil, for deep-frying		

Cook shrimp crackers, in 3 to 4 batches, in hot (375°F, 190°C) cooking oil for 15 to 20 seconds until puffed. Remove quickly to paper towels to drain. Makes about 4 cups (1 L).

1 cup (250 mL): 153 Calories; 10.6 g Total Fat (2 g Mono, 5.5 g Poly, 2.6 g Sat); 0 mg Cholesterol; 14 g Carbohydrate; 1 g Fibre; 2 g Protein; 180 mg Sodium

Pictured on page 107.

Note: Uncooked shrimp crackers can be purchased at Asian grocery stores. These are small hard discs about 1/2 inch (12 mm) in diameter that puff to about 5 times their size when cooked. Not to be confused with shrimp crackers also available in Asian grocery stores that are already cooked.

Ham And Chicken Rolls

These easy-to-make spirals are attractive and very flavourful.
Serve with Sweet And Sour Sauce, page 15.

Boneless, skinless chicken breast halves (4 oz., 113 g, each)	4	4
Slices of deli ham, halved lengthwise	4	4
Chinese five-spice powder	1/2 tsp.	2 mL
Garlic clove, minced (or 1/4 tsp., 1 mL, powder)	1	1
Salt	1/4 tsp.	1 mL
All-purpose flour	1 tbsp.	15 mL
Water	1 tbsp.	15 mL
Spring roll wrappers (6 inch, 15 cm, square)	4	4
All-purpose flour	3 tbsp.	50 mL
Large eggs, fork-beaten	1 – 2	1 – 2

Cooking oil, for deep-frying

Pound chicken to 1/3 inch (1 cm) thickness. Lay 1 slice of ham over each piece of chicken.

Combine five-spice powder, garlic and salt in small cup. Sprinkle small amount over each ham slice. Roll up from short side.

Combine first amount of flour and water in separate small cup.

Lay 1 wrapper on work surface with 1 corner closest to you. Roll 1 chicken roll into second amount of flour then dip into egg. Place chicken roll across wrapper. Brush edges of wrapper with flour paste. Fold up 1 corner over filling. Fold in both sides. Roll up tightly to seal. Repeat with remaining chicken rolls and wrappers.

Deep-fry in hot (350°F, 175°C) cooking oil for about 5 minutes until golden and chicken is no longer pink inside. Cut each roll into four 1/2 inch (12 mm) slices, for a total of 16 slices.

1 slice: 91 Calories; 2.8 g Total Fat (1.3 g Mono, 0.6 g Poly, 0.6 g Sat); 35 mg Cholesterol; 6 g Carbohydrate; trace Fibre; 9 g Protein; 200 mg Sodium

Pictured on page 17.

Soy Dipping Sauce

This salty, dark brown sauce is perfect for dipping or for
drizzling over savoury dim sum selections.

Soy sauce	1/3 cup	75 mL
Smooth peanut butter	1 1/2 tbsp.	25 mL
White vinegar	1 tbsp.	15 mL
Brown sugar, packed	1 tbsp.	15 mL
Granulated sugar	1 tsp.	5 mL
Cayenne pepper	1/4 tsp.	1 mL
Garlic powder	1/8 tsp.	0.5 mL

Measure all 7 ingredients into small saucepan. Heat and stir on medium for 3 to 4 minutes until boiling and sugar is dissolved. Makes a scant 1/2 cup (125 mL).

2 tbsp. (30 mL): 68 Calories; 3 g Total Fat (1.4 g Mono, 0.8 g Poly, 0.6 g Sat); 0 mg Cholesterol; 8 g Carbohydrate; trace Fibre; 4 g Protein; 1415 mg Sodium

Pictured on page 35.

Hot Mustard Sauce

Watch out! This smooth, yellow paste is fiery hot!
Serve this with Deep-Fried Wontons, page 14. Easy to increase.

Dry mustard, stir to break up any lumps before measuring	2 tbsp.	30 mL
White vinegar	2 tsp.	10 mL
Cold water, approximately	2 tsp.	10 mL

Stir mustard and vinegar in small cup.

Add water, a little at a time, stirring until smooth, fairly thin paste. Let stand for 30 minutes to blend flavours. Makes about 1 tbsp. (15 mL).

1/4 tsp. (1 mL): 9 Calories; 0.5 g Total Fat (0.4 g Mono, 0.1 g Poly, trace Sat); 0 mg Cholesterol; 1 g Carbohydrate; trace Fibre; trace Protein; trace Sodium

Pictured on page 17.

Variation: This can be toned down by adding sour cream if you find it too hot for your liking.

Dim Sum

Dim sum, meaning "touch your heart," refers to an age-old Chinese tea time tradition where a variety of little snacks are served in steamer baskets or on small plates. Dim sum dishes usually consist of steamed or fried dumplings, pan-fried cakes, spring rolls, baked buns, as well as many other delicious selections. And we can't forget to mention the delicate dim sum desserts such as sweet cakes and custard tarts. We hope these recipes will touch your heart!

Cantonese Har Gow

Also known as shrimp dumplings, these are traditional fare for dim sum and are so, so good! A time-consuming recipe, it is best saved for special occasions.

SHRIMP FILLING

Raw shrimp, peeled and deveined, blotted dry, finely chopped	6 oz.	170 g
Finely chopped water chestnuts	1 1/2 tbsp.	25 mL
Green onion, finely sliced	1	1
Finely grated peeled gingerroot	1/4 tsp.	1 mL
Cornstarch	2 tsp.	10 mL
Dry sherry	1 tsp.	5 mL
Soy sauce	1 tsp.	5 mL
Sesame oil	1/2 tsp.	2 mL
Brown sugar, packed	1/4 tsp.	1 mL
Salt	1/8 tsp.	0.5 mL

TRANSLUCENT WRAPPERS

Wheat starch	1/2 cup	125 mL
Tapioca (or corn) starch	1/4 cup	60 mL
Salt	1/2 tsp.	2 mL
Boiling water	1/2 cup	125 mL

(continued on next page)

Cooking oil	1 tbsp.	15 mL
Parchment paper squares, 5 inch (12.5 cm) size	17	17
Suey choy (Chinese cabbage) leaves (or parchment paper), to line steamer	2	2

Shrimp Filling: Combine first 4 ingredients in small bowl.

Add next 6 ingredients. Stir until combined. Cover. Chill until ready to use.

Translucent Wrappers: Stir wheat starch, tapioca starch and salt in medium bowl.

Add boiling water all at once. Immediately stir until combined and very thick.

Add cooking oil, 1 tsp. (5 mL) at a time, stirring well after each addition. Knead with greased hands for 3 to 4 minutes until dough is very smooth and soft. Divide in half. Shape each half into cylinder about 8 inches (20 cm) long. Keep rolls covered with greased plastic wrap to prevent drying out. Cut 1 roll into 8 pieces. Roll out each piece between 2 squares of parchment paper to 3 inch (7.5 cm) circle. Peel off top paper. Place 1 1/2 tsp. (7 mL) filling in centre of wrapper. Fold dough over filling using paper to assist in rolling. Press edge together firmly. With greased hands, make 6 to 7 small pleats along edges to seal. Stand upright on paper. Repeat with remaining dough, filling and paper, keeping dumplings covered with greased plastic wrap to prevent drying out.

Line bottom of bamboo steamer with suey choy leaves. Place dumplings on leaves, in batches, not touching side or each other. Set steamer on rack over boiling water in wok or Dutch oven. Cover. Cook for about 8 minutes until filling is pink and wrapper is transparent. Do not overcook. Makes 16 dumplings.

1 dumpling: 43 Calories; 1.2 g Total Fat (0.6 g Mono, 0.4 g Poly, 0.1 g Sat); 12 mg Cholesterol; 6 g Carbohydrate; trace Fibre; 2 g Protein; 127 mg Sodium

Pictured on page 35.

To Make Ahead: Cover dumplings with greased waxed paper. Chill for 2 to 3 hours before steaming. Uncooked dumplings may be frozen before cooking if fresh (not previously frozen) shrimp were used in the filling. Steam dumplings from frozen state for 9 to 10 minutes.

Chinese Vegetable Rolls

These crisp, deep-fried rolls are full of fresh, chunky vegetables. Serve with Plum Sauce, page 23, or Soy Dipping Sauce, page 27, for a delicious treat.

OYSTER SAUCE

Cold water	1 tbsp.	15 mL
Soy sauce	1 tbsp.	15 mL
Oyster sauce	1 tbsp.	15 mL
Dry sherry	2 tsp.	10 mL
Sesame oil	1 tsp.	5 mL
Cornstarch	2 tsp.	10 mL
Chinese dried mushrooms	6	6
Boiling water, to cover		
Cooking oil	1 tbsp.	15 mL
Chopped green onion	3/4 cup	175 mL
Fresh bean sprouts	2 cups	500 mL
Salt	1/4 tsp.	1 mL
Dry sherry	1 tsp.	5 mL
Cooking oil	1 tbsp.	15 mL
Garlic cloves, minced (or 1/2 tsp., 2 mL, powder)	2	2
Finely grated peeled gingerroot	1/2 tsp.	2 mL
Finely shredded Suey choy (Chinese cabbage), packed	1 cup	250 mL
Grated carrot	2/3 cup	150 mL
Finely chopped canned bamboo shoots	1/4 cup	60 mL
Finely chopped water chestnuts	1/4 cup	60 mL
All-purpose flour	2 tbsp.	30 mL
Water	2 tbsp.	30 mL
Egg roll wrappers	12	12
Cooking oil, for deep-frying		

(continued on next page)

Oyster Sauce: Stir first 6 ingredients in small dish until smooth. Set aside.

Put mushrooms into small bowl. Add boiling water. Let stand for 20 minutes until softened. Drain. Remove and discard stems. Slice caps thinly. Set aside.

Heat wok or large frying pan on medium-high until very hot. Add first amount of cooking oil. Add green onion, bean sprouts, salt and sherry. Stir-fry for 1 minute. Turn into colander to drain and cool.

Heat second amount of cooking oil in wok. Add next 6 ingredients and sliced mushrooms. Stir-fry for about 2 minutes until cabbage is softened. Stir sauce. Add to cabbage mixture. Heat and stir until boiling and thickened. Turn out onto plate to cool. Combine with bean sprouts mixture in medium bowl.

Combine flour and water in small cup until smooth and consistency of medium-thin paste.

Lay 1 wrapper on work surface with 1 corner closest to you. Keep unused wrappers covered with damp tea towel to prevent drying out. Place about 3 tbsp. (50 mL) vegetable mixture in centre of wrapper. Brush 2 adjoining sides of wrapper with flour mixture. Fold up 1 corner over filling. Fold in both sides. Roll up tightly to seal. Repeat with remaining filling and wrappers, keeping filled rolls covered with damp tea towel.

Deep-fry, 4 at a time, in hot (350°F, 175°C) cooking oil for about 2 minutes, turning once, until crisp and golden. Remove to paper towels to drain. Makes 12 rolls.

1 roll: 189 Calories, 7.9 g Total Fat (4.3 g Mono, 2.4 g Poly, 0.7 g Sat), 3 mg Cholesterol, 25 g Carbohydrate; 1 g Fibre; 5 g Protein; 449 mg Sodium

Pictured on page 35.

To Make Ahead: Freeze cooked rolls in airtight container. Arrange on ungreased baking sheet. Heat in 350°F (175°C) oven until heated through.

Paré Pointer
Where there's a wok, there's a way.

Shrimp Tail Purses

Shrimp tails poke out of these golden bundles. The fresh ginger accents the crisp Chinese cabbage and crunchy water chestnuts.

PORK FILLING		
Egg white (large)	1	1
Lean ground pork	4 oz.	113 g
Finely grated peeled gingerroot	1/2 tsp.	2 mL
Garlic clove, minced (or 1/4 tsp., 1 mL, powder)	1	1
Cornstarch	1 tbsp.	15 mL
Soy sauce	1 1/2 tsp.	7 mL
Dry sherry	1 1/2 tsp.	7 mL
Sesame oil (optional)	1 tsp.	5 mL
Suey choy (Chinese cabbage) leaf, shredded	1	1
Finely chopped water chestnuts	1/4 cup	60 mL
Finely chopped green onion	1 tbsp.	15 mL
Wonton wrappers	22 – 24	22 – 24
Raw medium shrimp (tails intact), peeled and deveined, blotted dry	22 – 24	22 – 24
Suey choy (Chinese cabbage) leaves (or parchment paper), to line steamer	2	2

Pork Filling: Beat egg white with fork in small bowl. Add next 10 ingredients. Mix. Makes 1 1/4 cups (300 mL) filling.

Place generous 2 tsp. (10 mL) filling in centre of each wrapper. Place 1 shrimp with tail up in pork mixture. Gather up sides of wrapper around filling, making small pleats and leaving top slightly open and tail showing. Gently squeeze centre of purse to pack filling. Tap "purses" gently on work surface to flatten bottom slightly.

Line bottom of large bamboo steamer with second amount of suey choy leaves. Place purses on leaves, in batches, not touching side or each other. Set steamer on rack over rapidly boiling water in wok or Dutch oven. Cover. Cook for about 12 minutes until pork is cooked and shrimp is pink. Makes about 24 purses.

1 purse: 40 Calories; 0.5 g Total Fat (0.2 g Mono, 0.1 g Poly, 0.1 g Sat); 13 mg Cholesterol; 5 g Carbohydrate; trace Fibre; 3 g Protein; 79 mg Sodium

Pictured on page 18.

Steamed Dim Sims

These small, pleated parcels have a spicy shrimp filling.
Serve with Sweet And Sour Sauce, page 15.

PORK AND SHRIMP FILLING

Chinese dried mushrooms	6	6
Boiling water, to cover		
Raw medium shrimp, peeled and deveined, chopped	1/2 lb.	225 g
Ground pork	4 oz.	113 g
Finely chopped cabbage	1/2 cup	125 mL
Garlic cloves, minced (or 1/2 tsp., 2 mL, powder)	2	2
Chopped fresh cilantro (optional)	2 tbsp.	30 mL
Hoisin sauce	2 tbsp.	30 mL
Finely grated peeled gingerroot	1 tsp.	5 mL
Soy sauce	1 tbsp.	15 mL
Chinese barbecue sauce	1 tbsp.	15 mL
Sesame oil	1 tsp.	5 mL
Wonton wrappers	48	48
Large egg, fork-beaten	1	1

Pork And Shrimp Filling: Put mushrooms into small bowl. Add boiling water. Let stand for 20 minutes until softened. Drain. Remove and discard stems. Chop caps finely. Put into large bowl.

Add next 10 ingredients. Mix well. Makes about 2 cups (500 mL) filling.

Place 2 tsp. (10 mL) filling in centre of each wrapper. Brush edges lightly with egg. Gather up sides of wrapper around filling, making small pleats and leaving top slightly open. Line bottom of large bamboo steamer with parchment paper. Poke small holes all over paper. Place dim sims on paper, in batches, not touching side or each other. Set steamer on rack over simmering water in wok or Dutch oven. Cover. Cook for about 10 minutes until filling is firm and wrapper is soft. Makes 48 appetizers.

1 appetizer: 40 Calories; 0.9 g Total Fat (0.3 g Mono, 0.2 g Poly, 0.3 g Sat); 12 mg Cholesterol; 6 g Carbohydrate; trace Fibre; 2 g Protein; 95 mg Sodium

Tofu And Shrimp Drops

These little round balls are packed with a soft, well-seasoned filling.
Tone down the heat in the aftertaste by serving with Sweet
And Sour Sauce, page 15, or Plum Sauce, page 23.

Firm tofu, drained, patted dry and cut into 8 pieces	4 oz.	113 g
Raw shrimp, peeled and deveined	5 oz.	140 g
All-purpose flour	1/4 cup	60 mL
Green onion, cut into 4 pieces	1	1
Finely grated peeled gingerroot	1 tsp.	5 mL
Oyster sauce	1 tbsp.	15 mL
Chili paste (sambal oelek)	1/2 tsp.	2 mL
Egg yolk (large)	1	1
Salt	1/8 tsp.	0.5 mL

Cooking oil, for deep-frying

Process first 9 ingredients in food processor using on/off motion for about 30 seconds until well mixed and paste-like consistency.

Drop by generous teaspoonfuls, about 5 at a time, into hot (375°F, 190°C) cooking oil. Cook for 1 1/2 to 2 minutes, stirring often, until golden brown. Remove to paper towels to drain. Makes about 30 drops.

1 drop: 36 Calories; 2.9 g Total Fat (1.5 g Mono, 1 g Poly, 0.3 g Sat); 13 mg Cholesterol; 1 g Carbohydrate; trace Fibre; 2 g Protein; 66 mg Sodium

1. Coconut Custard Tarts, page 43
2. Cocktail Buns, page 40
3. Cantonese Har Gow, page 28
4. Chinese Vegetable Rolls, page 30
5. Sesame Seed Balls, page 42
6. Soy Dipping Sauce, page 27
7. Pearl Balls, page 37

Props Courtesy Of: Kitchen Treasures
The Bay

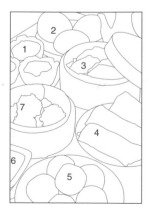

Pearl Balls

These pretty rice-coated meatballs have a unique, spiky look.

Long grain sweet (glutinous) rice	1 cup	250 mL
Cold water	4 cups	1 L
Lean ground pork	3/4 lb.	340 g
Chinese pork sausage, finely chopped (about 1 1/2 oz., 43 g)	1	1
Canned bamboo shoots, finely chopped	1/4 cup	60 mL
Water chestnuts, chopped	4	4
Cornstarch	1 tbsp.	15 mL
Soy sauce	1 tbsp.	15 mL
Sesame oil (optional)	2 tsp.	10 mL
Dry sherry	2 tsp.	10 mL
Suey choy (Chinese cabbage) leaves (or parchment paper), to line steamer	2	2

Soak rice in cold water in medium bowl for 2 hours. Drain.

Combine next 8 ingredients in separate medium bowl. Knead until sticky, soft and well mixed. Shape into 1 inch (2.5 cm) balls. Spread out rice on baking sheet in even layer. Roll meatballs in rice until coated.

Line bottom of bamboo steamer with suey choy leaves. Place meatballs 1 inch (2.5 cm) apart on leaves. Set steamer on rack over boiling water in wok or Dutch oven. Cover. Cook for 18 to 20 minutes until pork is cooked and rice is tender. Makes about 30 meatballs.

1 meatball: 54 Calories; 1.3 g Total Fat (0.6 g Mono, 0.1 g Poly, 0.4 g Sat); 8 mg Cholesterol; 7 g Carbohydrate; trace Fibre; 3 g Protein; 60 mg Sodium

Pictured on page 35.

1. Chinese Tomato Soup, page 45
2. Egg Flower Soup, page 52
3. Fish Ball Soup, page 44
4. Hot And Sour Soup, page 49
5. Oriental Noodle Soup, page 55

Props Courtesy Of: Kitchen Treasures

Steamed Pork Dumplings

*Traditionally known as Shui Mai, these dumplings are
classic dim sum fare. Top with a spot of red fish roe or caviar.*

Lean ground pork	8 oz.	225 g
Finely chopped green onion	2 tbsp.	30 mL
Soy sauce	1 1/2 tbsp.	25 mL
Hoisin sauce	2 tsp.	10 mL
Finely grated carrot	2 tbsp.	30 mL
Can of bamboo shoots (or water chestnuts), drained and finely chopped	8 oz.	227 mL
Finely grated peeled gingerroot	1 tsp.	5 mL
Garlic clove, minced (optional)	1	1
Egg white (large)	1	1
Round dumpling wrappers, thawed	20	20
Suey choy (Chinese cabbage) leaves (or parchment paper), to line steamer	2	2
DUMPLING HOT SAUCE		
Soy sauce	1/4 cup	60 mL
Sweet (or regular) chili sauce	2 tbsp.	30 mL
Vietnamese hot sauce	1/2 tsp.	2 mL

Combine first 9 ingredients in medium bowl. Knead until well mixed, sticky and soft.

Place 1 1/2 tbsp. (25 mL) filling in centre of each wrapper. Gather up wrapper around filling, making small pleats and leaving top slightly open. Gently squeeze centre of dumpling to pack filling. Tap dumplings gently on work surface to flatten bottom slightly.

Line bottom of large bamboo steamer with suey choy leaves. Place dumplings on leaves, in batches, not touching side or each other. Set steamer on rack over boiling water in wok or Dutch oven. Cover. Cook for about 15 minutes until pork is cooked.

Dumpling Hot Sauce: Stir all 3 ingredients in small cup. Makes scant 1/2 cup (125 mL) sauce. Serve with dumplings. Makes 20 dumplings.

1 dumpling with 1 tsp. (5 mL) sauce: 48 Calories; 0.8 g Total Fat (0.3 g Mono, 0.1 g Poly, 0.3 g Sat); 8 mg Cholesterol; 6 g Carbohydrate; trace Fibre; 4 g Protein; 391 mg Sodium

Pictured on page 18 and on back cover.

Basic Dough

This dough makes slightly sweet, light and fluffy buns.
Use for Cocktail Buns, page 40, and Sweet Buns, page 41.

Very warm water	1/3 cup	75 mL
Granulated sugar	1 tsp.	5 mL
Active dry yeast	2 tsp.	10 mL
Granulated sugar	1/3 cup	75 mL
Salt	1/2 tsp.	2 mL
Cooking oil	3 tbsp.	50 mL
Boiling water	1/4 cup	60 mL
Large egg, fork-beaten	1	1
White bread flour, approximately	2 1/4 cups	550 mL

Stir warm water and first amount of sugar in small dish until sugar is dissolved. Sprinkle yeast over top. Let stand for 10 minutes. Stir to dissolve yeast.

Stir second amount of sugar, salt and cooking oil in large bowl. Add boiling water. Stir until sugar is dissolved. Stir in egg and yeast mixture.

Slowly work in enough flour until soft dough forms. Turn out onto lightly floured surface. Knead for about 10 minutes until smooth and elastic. Place dough in large greased bowl, turning once to grease top. Cover with greased waxed paper and tea towel. Let stand in oven with light on and door closed for 1 1/2 to 2 hours until doubled in bulk. Punch dough down. Cover. Let rest for 5 minutes. Shape into 12 inch (30 cm) log. Cut into 12 pieces. Fill, shape and bake buns according to desired recipes. Makes 12 buns.

1 unfilled bun: 161 Calories; 4.4 g Total Fat (2.3 g Mono, 1.3 g Poly, 0.4 g Sat); 18 mg Cholesterol; 26 g Carbohydrate; trace Fibre; 4 g Protein; 105 mg Sodium

Pictured on page 35 (Cocktail Buns).

To Proof Overnight: Knead dough and place in large greased bowl, turning once to grease top. Cover with greased plastic wrap and chill overnight. Punch dough down. Cover. Let rest for 5 minutes. Fill and shape buns as desired.

Cocktail Buns

Also known as coconut buns, these have a sweet, buttery coconut filling.
This recipe fills 6 buns or 1/2 of Basic Dough recipe.

COCONUT FILLING		
Flake coconut	1 1/3 cups	325 mL
Granulated sugar	1 tbsp.	15 mL
Hard margarine (or butter), melted	2 tbsp.	30 mL
Egg yolk (large)	1	1
Prepared Basic Dough, page 39	1/2	1/2
EGG WASH		
Large egg	1	1
Water	1 tbsp.	15 mL
HONEY WASH		
Liquid honey	1 tbsp.	15 mL
Hot water	1 tbsp.	15 mL

Coconut Filling: Process coconut and sugar in blender or food processor until very fine. Turn into small bowl.

Stir in margarine and egg yolk until paste-like consistency. Makes scant 2/3 cup (150 mL) filling.

Divide dough into 6 portions. Press and stretch each portion into 5 x 3 inch (12.5 x 7.5 cm) oblong shape. Place rounded 1 1/2 tbsp. (25 mL) filling lengthwise along centre of each piece. Bring long sides up and over filling, pinching all edges together to seal. Place, seam-side down, on greased baking sheet. Cover with greased waxed paper and tea towel. Let stand in oven with light on and door closed for about 1 hour until doubled in size.

Egg Wash: Beat egg and water together with fork in small cup. Brush over buns. Bake in 350°F (175°C) oven for 15 to 18 minutes until golden brown.

Honey Wash: Combine honey and hot water in separate small cup. Brush over warm buns. Serve warm. Makes 6 buns.

1 bun: 316 Calories; 15.4 g Total Fat (5.6 g Mono, 2 g Poly, 6.6 g Sat); 90 mg Cholesterol; 39 g Carbohydrate; 1 g Fibre; 6 g Protein; 206 mg Sodium

Pictured on page 35.

To Make Ahead: Dough may be made the day before and stored, covered, in refrigerator overnight. Baked buns may be frozen and reheated, wrapped well in foil, in 350°F (175°C) oven for 15 minutes.

Sweet Buns

Sweetened red bean paste and lotus seed paste are available in Chinese food stores and they make delicious fillings in these soft, sweet buns.

Prepared Basic Dough, page 39	1	1
Sweetened red bean paste (see Note)	3/4 cup	175 mL
EGG WASH		
Large egg	1	1
Water	1 tbsp.	15 mL
HONEY WASH		
Liquid honey	1 tbsp.	15 mL
Hot water	1 tbsp.	15 mL

Divide dough into 12 portions. Press and stretch each portion into 4 inch (10 cm) circle.

Place rounded tablespoon of paste onto each circle. Bring dough up and over filling, pinching all edges together to seal. Shape into flattened discs. Place, seam-side down, 2 inches (5 cm) apart on greased baking sheet. Cover with greased waxed paper and tea towel. Let stand in oven with light on and door closed for about 1 hour until doubled in size.

Egg Wash: Beat egg and water together with fork in small cup. Brush over buns. Bake in 350°F (175°C) oven for 15 to 18 minutes until golden brown.

Honey Wash: Combine honey and hot water in separate small cup. Brush over warm buns. Serve warm. Makes 12 buns.

1 bun: 196 Calories; 4.8 g Total Fat (2.4 g Mono, 1.4 g Poly, 0.6 g Sat); 36 mg Cholesterol; 33 g Carbohydrate; 1 g Fibre; 5 g Protein; 111 mg Sodium

Note: Lotus seed paste can be substituted for the sweet red bean paste. If you'd like to make 6 of each, use 6 tbsp. (100 mL) of each paste. To differentiate, brush on an "S" or "X" with Egg Wash on top of appropriate buns.

To Make Ahead: Dough may be made the day before and stored, covered, in refrigerator overnight. Baked buns may be frozen and reheated, wrapped well in foil, in 350°F (175°C) oven for 15 minutes.

Sesame Seed Balls

These balls of golden pastry are coated in sesame seeds and have a sweet, sticky filling. These will definitely become a favourite!

Brown sugar, packed	3/4 cup	175 mL
Water	3/4 cup	175 mL
Glutinous rice flour	2 1/4 cups	550 mL
Lotus seed paste	1/2 cup	125 mL
Sesame seeds	1/2 cup	125 mL

Cooking oil, for deep-frying

Heat brown sugar and water in large saucepan on medium for about 4 minutes, stirring occasionally, until boiling and sugar is dissolved. Remove from heat.

Add 1 1/2 cups (375 mL) rice flour. Stir until smooth. Add remaining rice flour, 2 tbsp. (30 mL) at a time, stirring well after each addition, until mixture leaves side of saucepan. Coat hands in rice flour. Form about 1 tbsp. (15 mL) dough into 1 1/2 inch (3.8 cm) ball. Poke your finger into centre to form indentation. Keep remaining dough covered with damp tea towel to prevent drying out.

Fill indentation with 1 tsp. (5 mL) lotus seed paste. Bring edges together. Press to seal well. Roll into ball.

Put sesame seeds into small bowl. Dampen outside of ball with water. Roll in sesame seeds until completely coated. Repeat with remaining dough, filling and sesame seeds.

Deep-fry, several at a time, in hot (325°F, 160°C) cooking oil for 8 to 10 minutes. As they cook, occasionally hold balls against side of deep fryer or wok with 2 chopsticks or heatproof spatula to help them fill with air and float to top. They should be deep golden brown and about 2 times bigger than original size. Remove to paper towels to drain. Makes 22 balls.

1 ball: 163 Calories; 6.6 g Total Fat (3.5 g Mono, 2.2 g Poly, 0.6 g Sat); 0 mg Cholesterol; 25 g Carbohydrate; 1 g Fibre; 2 g Protein; 5 mg Sodium

Pictured on page 35.

Coconut Custard Tarts

Smooth, pale yellow custard and golden, chewy coconut are encased in a flaky pastry. These decadent dim sum treats can easily be made ahead of time.

COCONUT CUSTARD FILLING

Granulated sugar	3/4 cup	175 mL
Water	1/2 cup	125 mL
Salt	1/8 tsp.	0.5 mL
Large eggs	4	4
Cold water	1/4 cup	60 mL
Cornstarch	1 1/2 tbsp.	25 mL
Flake coconut	1 cup	250 mL

Pastry for a 2 crust pie, your own or
a mix

Coconut Custard Filling: Combine sugar, water and salt in small saucepan. Bring to a boil. Boil for 1 minute. Cool completely.

Beat eggs in medium bowl until frothy.

Stir cold water into cornstarch in small dish. Add to eggs. Beat until mixed. Add cooled sugar mixture. Beat together.

Stir in coconut. Makes 2 1/4 cups (550 mL) filling.

Roll out pastry on lightly floured surface to 1/8 inch (3 mm) thickness. Cut into 4 1/2 inch (11 cm) circles with cutter. Line ungreased muffin cups with pastry. Pinch or ruffle top edge that extends over cup. Stir filling. Fill each cup to within 1/2 inch (12 mm) of edge. Bake on bottom rack in 375°F (190°C) oven for about 30 minutes until custard is rounded and coconut is starting to turn golden. Do not overcook. Let stand in pan on wire rack to cool for 10 minutes. Carefully remove individual tarts to serve warm. Makes 12 tarts.

1 tart: 219 Calories; 10.7 g Total Fat (4 g Mono, 1.1 g Poly, 4.6 g Sat); 72 mg Cholesterol; 28 g Carbohydrate; trace Fibre; 3 g Protein; 199 mg Sodium

Pictured on page 35.

To Make Ahead: Freeze baked tarts in airtight container. Arrange on ungreased baking sheet. Heat in 325°F (160°C) oven for about 20 minutes until heated through. Serve warm.

Fish Ball Soup

The delicate fish balls and fresh green pea pods
give this soup a unique flavour and appearance.

FISH BALLS

Fresh (or frozen, thawed and blotted dry) white fish fillets, cubed	8 oz.	225 g
Finely chopped green onion	2 tbsp.	30 mL
Bacon slice, cooked crisp and crumbled (or 1 tbsp., 15 mL, real bacon bits)	1	1
Chili paste (sambal oelek), optional	1/4 tsp.	1 mL
Salt	1/4 tsp.	1 mL
Pepper	1/16 tsp.	0.5 mL

SOUP

Prepared chicken broth	6 cups	1.5 L
Dry sherry	2 tbsp.	30 mL
Soy sauce	1 tbsp.	15 mL
Slivered fresh pea pods	1 cup	250 mL

GARNISH

Cooking oil	2 tsp.	10 mL
Garlic cloves, minced	3	3

Fish Balls: Process fish in blender or food processor until pasty and smooth. Turn into small bowl.

Add next 5 ingredients. Mix. Shape into 1 inch (2.5 cm) balls, using 1/2 tbsp. (7 mL) for each. Makes about 20 fish balls.

Soup: Combine first 3 ingredients in large saucepan. Bring to a boil. Drop in fish balls. Cook for about 3 minutes until firm and white.

Add pea pods. Simmer for about 30 seconds until bright green and tender-crisp.

Garnish: Heat cooking oil in small saucepan or frying pan on medium. Add garlic. Cook for about 2 minutes, stirring constantly, until nicely browned. Sprinkle over individual servings. Makes 7 cups (1.75 L). Serves 6.

1 serving: 127 Calories; 5.5 g Total Fat (2.4 g Mono, 1.6 g Poly, 1 g Sat); 23 mg Cholesterol; 4 g Carbohydrate; 1 g Fibre; 14 g Protein; 1122 mg Sodium

Pictured on page 36.

Chinese Tomato Soup

This soup contains an appealing variety of fresh ingredients. The subtle flavour of the broth is light and very pleasant.

Prepared chicken broth	5 cups	1.25 L
Sliced onion	1 cup	250 mL
Medium tomatoes, skins removed (see Tip, below), cut into 8 wedges each	3	3
Granulated sugar	1/2 tsp.	2 mL
Salt	1/4 tsp.	1 mL
Pepper	1/8 tsp.	0.5 mL
Fresh pea pods, cut in half	1 cup	250 mL
Large egg	1	1
Green onions, sliced	2	2

Combine first 6 ingredients in large saucepan. Bring to a boil. Reduce heat to medium. Cook for about 15 minutes, stirring occasionally, until onion is softened.

Add pea pods.

Beat egg with fork in 1 cup (250 mL) liquid measure. Add egg to broth mixture in thin stream, constantly stirring in circular motion until fine egg threads form.

Sprinkle individual servings with green onion. Makes about 6 cups (1.5 L). Serves 6.

1 serving: 51 Calories; 1.4 g Total Fat (0.5 g Mono, 0.3 g Poly, 0.4 g Sat); 36 mg Cholesterol; 8 g Carbohydrate; 2 g Fibre; 3 g Protein; 442 mg Sodium

Pictured on page 36.

 To remove skin from tomatoes, cut small 'x' on bottom of tomatoes. Put into boiling water in large saucepan for 30 to 60 seconds. Plunge into ice water until cold. Skin will lift up at cut for easy peeling.

Vegetarian Wonton Soup

An intensely flavoured broth surrounds fresh wontons and colourful green onions. Stuffed with bean threads and vegetables, the wontons have a bit of a crunch and they make a delicious addition to the soup. Use half of the wontons in the soup and freeze the other half for later—or use them in the variation below.

WONTONS

Chinese dried mushrooms	3	3
Boiling water, to cover		
Sesame (or cooking) oil	2 tsp.	10 mL
Finely chopped onion	1/4 cup	60 mL
Grated carrot	1/4 cup	60 mL
Garlic clove, minced (or 1/4 tsp., 1 mL, powder)	1	1
Fresh spinach, stems removed, lightly packed (about 6 oz., 170 g)	3 cups	750 mL
Can of water chestnuts, drained and finely chopped	8 oz.	227 mL
Bean threads (or rice vermicelli)	2 oz.	57 g
Boiling water, to cover		
Prepared black bean sauce	1/4 cup	60 mL
Wonton wrappers	80	80

VEGETARIAN BROTH

Cans of condensed vegetable broth (10 oz., 284 mL, each)	3	3
Water	3 1/2 cups	875 mL
Dry sherry	1 tbsp.	15 mL
Soy sauce	1 tbsp.	15 mL
Gingerroot slices (1/4 inch, 6 mm, thick), peeled	2	2
Boiling water	12 cups	3 L
Salt	1 tbsp.	15 mL
Green onions, cut julienne	2	2

(continued on next page)

Wontons: Put mushrooms into small bowl. Add boiling water. Let stand for 20 minutes until softened. Drain. Remove and discard stems. Chop caps finely. Put into medium bowl. Set aside.

Heat large frying pan on medium until hot. Add sesame oil. Add onion, carrot and garlic. Cook for about 5 minutes, stirring occasionally, until softened.

Add spinach and water chestnuts. Cook for about 4 minutes, stirring several times, until liquid is evaporated and mixture appears dry. Add to mushrooms.

Break bean threads into separate small bowl. Add boiling water. Let stand for 2 minutes. Drain well. Add to spinach mixture.

Add black bean sauce. Stir well to combine.

1. Lay 1 wrapper on work surface with 1 corner closest to you. Keep unused wrappers covered with damp tea towel to prevent drying out. Place about 1 1/2 tsp. (7 mL) filling in centre of wrapper. Brush adjacent edges of wrapper with water. 2. Fold up 1 corner to meet opposite corner, forming triangle. Press edges together very firmly to seal. Brush opposite corners with water. 3. Bring opposite corners together under filling. Press together firmly. Repeat with remaining filling and wrappers, keeping filled wontons covered with damp tea towels. Makes 80 wontons.

Vegetarian Broth: Combine first 5 ingredients in large saucepan. Bring to a boil. Reduce heat to medium-low. Cover. Simmer for 5 minutes. Remove and discard ginger. Makes 10 cups (2.5 L).

Cook 1/2 of wontons in boiling water and salt in large uncovered pot or Dutch oven for 2 to 3 minutes until tender. Drain. Add to hot broth.

Add green onion. Serves 8.

1 serving: 178 Calories; 2.3 g Total Fat (0.9 g Mono, 0.7 g Poly, 0.5 g Sat); 4 mg Cholesterol; 31 g Carbohydrate; 1 g Fibre; 8 g Protein; 1386 mg Sodium

DEEP-FRIED VEGETARIAN WONTONS: Deep-fry wontons from fresh or frozen state in hot (375°F, 190°C) cooking oil for about 1 minute until golden. Remove to paper towels to drain. Serve with Sweet And Sour Sauce, page 15, or Plum Sauce, page 23.

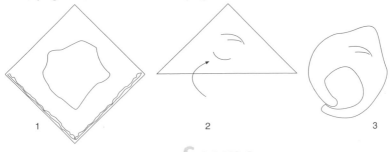

Soups

Wor Wonton Soup

A healthy, filling soup with delicate, moist wontons, tasty shrimp and fresh vegetables. Serve immediately or the wontons will soften.

Chinese dried mushrooms	2	2
Boiling water	1 cup	250 mL
Cans of condensed chicken broth (10 oz., 284 mL, each)	3	3
Water	3 cups	750 mL
Coarsely grated carrot	2 tbsp.	30 mL
Boneless pork loin, cut julienne into 1 1/2 inch (3.8 cm) lengths	4 oz.	113 g
Raw medium shrimp, peeled and deveined	12	12
Fresh pea pods, cut in half	12	12
Shredded spinach, lightly packed	1/2 cup	125 mL
Green onions, sliced	2	2
Wontons, page 46	20	20
Boiling water	12 cups	3 L

Put mushrooms into small bowl. Add first amount of boiling water. Let stand for 20 minutes until softened. Strain through fine cloth or several layers of cheesecloth, reserving liquid. Remove and discard stems. Slice caps thinly.

Combine reserved liquid, mushrooms and next 4 ingredients in large pot or Dutch oven. Bring to a boil. Reduce heat. Cover. Boil gently for about 5 minutes until pork is tender.

Add shrimp, pea pods, spinach and green onion. Cover. Boil gently for about 4 minutes until shrimp are pink and pea pods are tender-crisp.

Add wontons to second amount of boiling water in large saucepan. Boil gently, uncovered, for about 3 minutes, stirring gently occasionally, until wrapper clings to filling and filling is heated through. Drain. Add wontons to hot broth. Serve immediately, ensuring each bowl gets 3 or 4 wontons and 2 shrimp. Makes about 9 cups (2.25 L). Serves 6.

1 serving: 201 Calories; 4 g Total Fat (1.6 g Mono, 0.8 g Poly, 1.2 g Sat); 49 mg Cholesterol; 21 g Carbohydrate; 1 g Fibre; 20 g Protein; 1222 mg Sodium

Pictured on page 18 and on back cover.

WONTON SOUP: Add sliced fresh mushrooms and green onion to simmering prepared chicken broth. Cook wontons in separate saucepan, then add to chicken broth. Serve immediately.

Soups

Hot And Sour Soup

This simple soup makes a stimulating start to your meal. A gentle heat
and a mild sour tang add to the complex flavours of the broth.

Prepared chicken broth	6 cups	1.5 L
Boneless pork loin, cut julienne into 1 1/2 inch (3.8 cm) lengths	7 oz.	200 g
Sliced fresh white mushrooms	1 cup	250 mL
Water	1/2 cup	125 mL
Cornstarch	2 tbsp.	30 mL
White vinegar	3 tbsp.	50 mL
Soy sauce	2 tbsp.	30 mL
Chili paste (sambal oelek)	2 tsp.	10 mL
Pepper	1/4 tsp.	1 mL
Large egg	1	1
Green onions, sliced	2	2

Bring broth to a boil in large saucepan. Add pork. Return to a boil. Reduce heat. Cover. Boil gently for about 5 minutes until pork is tender.

Add mushrooms. Cover. Simmer for 10 minutes.

Stir water into cornstarch in small bowl. Add next 4 ingredients. Stir into pork mixture until boiling and slightly thickened.

Beat egg with fork in 1 cup (250 mL) liquid measure. Add egg to pork mixture in thin stream, constantly stirring in circular motion until fine egg threads form.

Sprinkle individual servings with green onion. Makes about 7 cups (1.75 L). Serves 6.

1 serving: 121 Calories; 4.3 g Total Fat (1.8 g Mono, 0.6 g Poly, 1.4 g Sat); 56 mg Cholesterol; 5 g Carbohydrate; trace Fibre; 14 g Protein; 1199 mg Sodium

Pictured on page 36.

Variation: Add 1/2 cup (125 mL) diced firm tofu and heat through.

Pork Vegetable Soup

Tender slices of pork and tender-crisp vegetables are dispersed
throughout this light, flavourful broth.

Chinese dried mushrooms	4	4
Boiling water, to cover		
Pork shoulder steak, cut into short thin strips	8 oz.	225 g
Cornstarch	1 tbsp.	15 mL
Cooking oil	1 tbsp.	15 mL
Cans of condensed chicken broth (10 oz., 284 mL, each)	2	2
Water	2 cups	500 mL
Thinly sliced small carrots	1/2 cup	125 mL
Diced celery	1/4 cup	60 mL
Sliced canned bamboo shoots	1/4 cup	60 mL
Finely chopped peeled gingerroot	1 tsp.	5 mL
Fresh pea pods	3/4 cup	175 mL
Chopped bok choy	1/2 cup	125 mL
Green onion, thinly sliced	1	1
Dry sherry	1 tbsp.	15 mL
Water	2 tbsp.	30 mL
Cornstarch	1 tbsp.	15 mL

Put mushrooms into small bowl. Add boiling water. Let stand for 20 minutes until softened. Drain. Remove and discard stems. Slice caps thinly. Set aside.

Coat pork with first amount of cornstarch.

Heat large saucepan on medium-high until hot. Add cooking oil. Add pork. Stir-fry for about 4 minutes until browned.

Add next 6 ingredients and mushrooms. Bring to a boil, stirring often. Reduce heat to medium. Boil gently, uncovered, for about 10 minutes until vegetables are tender.

(continued on next page)

Soups

Add next 4 ingredients. Simmer for about 2 minutes until pea pods are tender-crisp.

Stir third amount of water into second amount of cornstarch in small cup. Stir into soup, stirring constantly, until slightly thickened. Makes about 6 cups (1.5 L). Serves 6.

1 serving: 175 Calories; 10.2 g Total Fat (4.9 g Mono, 1.7 g Poly, 2.8 g Sat); 28 mg Cholesterol; 8 g Carbohydrate; 1 g Fibre; 12 g Protein; 673 mg Sodium

CHICKEN VEGETABLE SOUP: Omit pork. Add same amount of boneless, skinless chicken breast strips.

Egg Garnish

*These pale yellow, delicate strips of egg make
a delicious and interesting addition to almost any soup.
They are particularly good in Vegetarian Wonton Soup,
page 46, and Wor Wonton Soup, page 48.*

Large egg	1	1
Water	1 tbsp.	15 mL
Cooking oil	1/2 tsp.	2 mL

Beat all 3 ingredients in small bowl. Pour into greased non-stick frying pan, allowing egg mixture to spread. Cook on medium-low, without stirring, until firm. Turn out onto cutting board. Roll up tightly, jelly roll-style. Cut into 1/4 inch (6 mm) thick slices. Serve strips in soup. Makes about 1/4 cup (60 mL).

2 tbsp. (30 mL): 47 Calories; 3.7 g Total Fat (1.6 g Mono, 0.7 g Poly, 0.9 g Sat); 108 mg Cholesterol; trace Carbohydrate; 0 g Fibre; 3 g Protein; 32 mg Sodium

---

Paré Pointer
Wok with me, will you?

Egg Flower Soup

Also known as Egg Drop Soup, this soup has thready strands in an abstract flower shape.

Prepared chicken broth	6 cups	1.5 L
Gingerroot slices (1/4 inch, 6 mm, thick), peeled	4	4
Thinly sliced fresh shiitake (or brown) mushrooms	1/2 cup	125 mL
Light-coloured soy sauce	1 tbsp.	15 mL
Water	2 tbsp.	30 mL
Cornstarch	1 tbsp.	15 mL
Salt	1/4 tsp.	1 mL
White (or black) pepper, just a pinch		
Large eggs	2	2
Green onions, sliced	2	2

Heat broth and ginger in large saucepan on high until boiling.

Add mushrooms and soy sauce. Reduce heat to medium-low. Simmer, uncovered, for 10 minutes. Remove and discard ginger.

Stir water into cornstarch in small cup. Add salt and pepper. Mix. Stir into broth until boiling and slightly thickened.

Beat eggs with fork in 1 cup (250 mL) liquid measure. Slowly drizzle egg into soup while stirring briskly in circular motion. Fine egg threads will form in circular "flower" shape. Stir in green onion. Serve immediately. Makes 6 1/4 cups (1.5 L). Serves 6.

1 serving: 81 Calories; 3.2 g Total Fat (1.3 g Mono, 0.5 g Poly, 0.9 g Sat); 72 mg Cholesterol; 5 g Carbohydrate; trace Fibre; 8 g Protein; 1115 mg Sodium

Pictured on page 36.

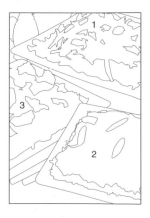

1. Ginger Beef, page 66
2. Braised Beef Curry, page 64
3. Beef Broccoli, page 56

Props Courtesy Of: Chintz & Company
Stokes

Oriental Noodle Soup

This soup's light broth surrounds chicken, pork and lots of noodles!

Boneless, skinless chicken breast half, diced	4 oz.	113 g
Boneless pork loin, diced	4 oz.	113 g
Grated carrot	1/4 cup	60 mL
Prepared chicken broth	6 cups	1.5 L
Chopped fresh white mushrooms	1/2 cup	125 mL
Diced cooked ham	1/2 cup	125 mL
Thinly sliced canned bamboo shoots	1/4 cup	60 mL
Fresh pea pods	18	18
Pepper, sprinkle		
Fine egg noodles	8 oz.	225 g
Boiling water	8 cups	2 L
Salt	2 tsp.	10 mL
Chili paste (sambal oelek), optional		
Hoisin sauce (optional)		

Put first 4 ingredients into large pot or Dutch oven. Bring to a boil. Reduce heat. Boil gently for 15 minutes, stirring occasionally.

Add next 5 ingredients. Boil gently for 5 minutes. Cover to keep warm.

Cook noodles in boiling water and salt in large uncovered saucepan for about 5 minutes until tender but firm. Drain. Divide noodles among 6 individual soup bowls.

Ladle soup over noodles. Flavour with chili paste or hoisin sauce as desired. Serves 6.

1 serving: 231 Calories; 4.6 g Total Fat (1.7 g Mono, 0.9 g Poly, 1.3 g Sat); 65 mg Cholesterol; 30 g Carbohydrate; 2 g Fibre; 17 g Protein; 830 mg Sodium

Pictured on page 36.

1. Mushroom Fried Rice, page 127
2. Moo Goo Gai Pan, page 78
3. Kung Pao Chicken, page 80

Props Courtesy Of: Cherison Enterprises Inc.
Chintz & Company

Beef Broccoli

This dish has a generous amount of beef and broccoli. The gingery, slightly sweet sauce can also be drizzled over rice or noodles.

MARINADE		
Finely grated peeled gingerroot	2 tbsp.	30 mL
Soy sauce	2 tbsp.	30 mL
Dry sherry	2 tbsp.	30 mL
Sesame oil (optional)	2 tsp.	10 mL
Granulated sugar	1 tsp.	5 mL
Garlic cloves, minced (or 1/4 – 3/4 tsp., 1 – 4 mL, powder)	1 – 3	1 – 3
Sirloin steak, cut across grain into 1/8 inch (3 mm) thick slices	3/4 lb.	340 g
Cooking oil	1 tbsp.	15 mL
Cooking oil	1 tbsp.	15 mL
Broccoli, stems cut into 1/8 inch (3 mm) thick slices (reserve florets), about 5 cups (1.25 L)	1 1/4 lbs.	560 g
Small onion, halved lengthwise and thinly sliced	1	1
Celery rib, cut into 1/4 inch (6 mm) slices	1	1
Prepared chicken broth	1/3 cup	75 mL
Water	2 tbsp.	30 mL
Cornstarch	4 tsp.	20 mL
Oyster sauce	1/3 cup	75 mL

Marinade: Combine first 6 ingredients in medium bowl.

Cut beef slices into 2 inch (5 cm) strips. Add to marinade. Stir until coated. Marinate at room temperature for 30 minutes.

Heat wok or large frying pan on medium-high until very hot. Add first amount of cooking oil. Add beef and marinade. Stir-fry for 2 to 3 minutes until beef is tender. Transfer to small bowl.

Add second amount of cooking oil to wok. Add broccoli stems, onion and celery. Stir-fry for 2 minutes. Add broccoli florets and broth. Stir. Cover. Cook for 3 to 4 minutes until broccoli is tender-crisp.

(continued on next page)

Main Dishes

Stir water into cornstarch in small cup. Add oyster sauce. Stir. Stir into broccoli mixture until boiling and thickened. Add beef. Stir until heated through. Makes about 5 1/2 cups (1.4 L). Serves 4.

1 serving: 302 Calories; 15.3 g Total Fat (7.5 g Mono, 2.6 g Poly, 3.7 g Sat); 42 mg Cholesterol; 20 g Carbohydrate; 4 g Fibre; 22 g Protein; 2625 mg Sodium

Pictured on page 53.

Sweet Beef

This tender beef has an irresistible smoky barbecue flavour.
The golden onions provide a nice contrast to the beef. A pricey treat.

Beef tenderloin	1 lb.	454 g
Ketchup	1/4 cup	60 mL
Worcestershire sauce	2 tbsp.	30 mL
Hoisin sauce	1 tbsp.	15 mL
Granulated sugar	1 tbsp.	15 mL
Peanut (or cooking) oil	1 tbsp.	15 mL
Medium onions, cut into 8 wedges each	2	2
Garlic clove, minced (or 1/4 tsp., 1 mL, powder)	1	1
Peanut (or cooking) oil	1 tbsp.	15 mL

Remove silver skin from tenderloin. Cut beef in half lengthwise. Cut each half across grain into 1/8 inch (3 mm) thick slices.

Combine next 4 ingredients in small bowl.

Heat wok or large frying pan on medium-high until very hot. Add first amount of peanut oil. Add onion and garlic. Stir-fry for about 3 minutes until onion is tender-crisp. Transfer to small bowl.

Add second amount of peanut oil to wok. Stir-fry beef, in 2 batches, for 2 to 3 minutes until browned. Combine beef, onion mixture and ketchup mixture in wok. Stir-fry for 1 to 2 minutes until very hot. Makes about 3 1/2 cups (875 mL). Serves 4.

1 serving: 301 Calories; 15.1 g Total Fat (6.3 g Mono, 2.7 g Poly, 4.2 g Sat); 57 mg Cholesterol; 16 g Carbohydrate; 1 g Fibre; 25 g Protein; 448 mg Sodium

Orange Beef And Broccoli

A colourful dish with a delicious sauce.

Orange juice	3/4 cup	175 mL
Cornstarch	1 tbsp.	15 mL
Soy sauce	3 tbsp.	50 mL
Granulated sugar	1 tbsp.	15 mL
White vinegar	1 tsp.	5 mL
Sirloin steak, cut across grain into 1/8 inch (3 mm) thick slices	1 lb.	454 g
Cooking oil	1 tbsp.	15 mL
Finely grated peeled gingerroot	2 tsp.	10 mL
Garlic clove, minced (or 1/4 tsp., 1 mL, powder)	1	1
Cooking oil	1 tbsp.	15 mL
Medium red onion, halved lengthwise and thinly sliced	1	1
Medium carrots, sliced paper-thin	2	2
Broccoli florets	2 cups	500 mL
Finely grated orange peel	1 tbsp.	15 mL
Medium orange, divided into segments and halved	1	1

Stir orange juice into cornstarch in small bowl. Add soy sauce, sugar and vinegar. Stir. Set aside.

Cut beef slices into 2 inch (5 cm) strips.

Heat wok or large frying pan on medium-high until very hot. Add 1 1/2 tsp. (7 mL) of first amount of cooking oil. Add ginger, garlic and 1/2 of beef. Stir-fry for 2 to 3 minutes until beef reaches desired doneness. Transfer to plate. Repeat with remaining first amount of cooking oil and beef. Transfer to plate.

Heat second amount of cooking oil in wok. Add onion and carrot. Stir-fry for about 3 minutes until almost tender-crisp.

Add broccoli and orange peel. Stir-fry until vegetables are tender.

(continued on next page)

Main Dishes

Add beef and orange. Stir cornstarch mixture. Stir into beef mixture until boiling and thickened. Makes 5 cups (1.25 L). Serves 4.

1 serving: 355 Calories; 17.4 g Total Fat (8.4 g Mono, 2.6 g Poly, 4.6 g Sat); 56 mg Cholesterol; 25 g Carbohydrate; 4 g Fibre; 26 g Protein; 873 mg Sodium

Pictured on page 125.

Oyster Sauce Beef

A stir-fry with a delicious rich, brown sauce. This has a smaller yield.

Prepared beef broth	1/4 cup	60 mL
Cornstarch	1 1/2 tsp.	7 mL
Oyster sauce	3 tbsp.	50 mL
Dry sherry	1 tbsp.	15 mL
Granulated sugar	1 tsp.	5 mL
Sesame oil	1 tsp.	5 mL
Sirloin steak, cut across grain into 1/8 inch (3 mm) thick slices	3/4 lb.	340 g
Cooking oil	1 tbsp.	15 mL
Sliced onion	1/2 cup	125 mL
Thinly sliced carrot	1/2 cup	125 mL
Thinly sliced canned bamboo shoots	1/4 cup	60 mL
Gingerroot slices (1/4 inch, 6 mm, thick), peeled	3	3
Green onions, cut into 2 inch (5 cm) pieces	3	3

Stir broth into cornstarch in small cup. Add next 4 ingredients. Stir. Set aside.

Cut beef slices into 2 inch (5 cm) strips.

Heat wok or large frying pan on medium-high until very hot. Add cooking oil. Add beef and onion. Stir-fry for 1 minute.

Add carrot, bamboo shoots and ginger. Stir-fry for 3 minutes.

Add green onion. Stir cornstarch mixture. Stir into beef mixture for about 1 minute until boiling and thickened. Remove and discard ginger. Makes about 2 cups (500 mL). Serves 3 to 4.

1 serving: 298 Calories; 16.5 g Total Fat (7.7 g Mono, 2.5 g Poly, 4.7 g Sat); 56 mg Cholesterol; 13 g Carbohydrate; 1 g Fibre; 23 g Protein; 1635 mg Sodium

Pictured on page 89.

Beef Chop Suey

This attractive mixture of thinly sliced beef and vegetables is bursting with flavour!

Prepared beef broth	1/3 cup	75 mL
Cornstarch	1 tbsp.	15 mL
Soy sauce	3 tbsp.	50 mL
Dry sherry	1 tbsp.	15 mL
Pepper	1/8 tsp.	0.5 mL
Sirloin steak, cut across grain into 1/8 inch (3 mm) thick slices	1/2 lb.	225 g
Cooking oil	2 tsp.	10 mL
Cooking oil	1 tbsp.	15 mL
Baby carrots, cut into 3 pieces each	10	10
Small onion, halved lengthwise and thinly sliced	1	1
Small red or green pepper, slivered	1	1
Sliced fresh white mushrooms	1 cup	250 mL
Can of bamboo shoots, drained and cut julienne	8 oz.	227 mL
Fresh bean sprouts	2 cups	500 mL

Stir broth into cornstarch in small bowl. Add soy sauce, sherry and pepper. Stir. Set aside.

Cut beef slices into 2 inch (5 cm) strips.

Heat wok or large frying pan on medium-high until very hot. Add first amount of cooking oil. Add beef. Stir-fry for 1 to 2 minutes until cooked to desired doneness. Transfer to separate small bowl.

Add second amount of cooking oil to wok. Add carrot and onion. Stir-fry for 1 to 2 minutes until almost tender-crisp.

Add red pepper, mushrooms and bamboo shoots. Stir-fry for 2 to 3 minutes until tender-crisp.

Add bean sprouts and beef. Stir-fry for about 1 minute until heated through. Stir cornstarch mixture. Stir into vegetable mixture until boiling and thickened. Makes 5 cups (1.25 L). Serves 4.

1 serving: 217 Calories; 11.2 g Total Fat (5.6 g Mono, 2.1 g Poly, 2.5 g Sat); 28 mg Cholesterol; 15 g Carbohydrate; 3 g Fibre; 15 g Protein; 900 mg Sodium

Main Dishes

Beef In Black Bean Sauce

This recipe uses the concentrated black bean sauce listed in the Glossary, page 8. Serve with rice.

Beef tenderloin	1 lb.	454 g
MARINADE		
Egg white (large)	1	1
Dry sherry	2 tbsp.	30 mL
Oyster sauce	1 tbsp.	15 mL
Granulated sugar	1 tsp.	5 mL
Garlic cloves, minced (or 1/2 tsp., 2 mL, powder)	2	2
Concentrated black bean sauce	1 tbsp.	15 mL
Water	1 tsp.	5 mL
Cornstarch	1 tsp.	5 mL
Cooking oil	1 1/2 tbsp.	25 mL
Green onions, cut into 1 inch (2.5 cm) pieces	8	8

Remove silver skin from tenderloin. Cut beef in half lengthwise. Cut each half across grain into 1/8 inch (3 mm) thick slices.

Marinade: Combine first 6 ingredients in medium bowl. Add beef. Stir until coated. Marinate at room temperature for 30 minutes.

Stir water into cornstarch in small cup. Set aside.

Heat wok or large frying pan on medium-high until very hot. Add cooking oil. Stir-fry beef mixture, in 2 batches, for about 2 minutes until beef is tender. Stir cornstarch mixture. Stir into beef mixture.

Add green onion. Heat and stir until boiling and thickened. Makes about 2 1/3 cups (575 mL). Serves 4.

1 serving: 250 Calories; 13.6 g Total Fat (6.4 g Mono, 2 g Poly, 3.4 g Sat); 57 mg Cholesterol; 4 g Carbohydrate; trace Fibre; 25 g Protein; 603 mg Sodium

Tender Beef And Cashews

You'll love the texture of this dish—soft beef and crunchy cashews.

MARINADE		
Soy sauce	1 tbsp.	15 mL
Garlic clove, minced (or 1/4 tsp., 1 mL, powder)	1	1
Dry sherry	2 tsp.	10 mL
Sesame oil	1/2 tsp.	2 mL
Granulated sugar	1/2 tsp.	2 mL
Pepper, sprinkle		
Beef tenderloin steak (3/4 inch, 2 cm, thick), cut across grain into 1/8 inch (3 mm) thick slices	3/4 lb.	340 g
Water	1/4 cup	60 mL
Cornstarch	1 tbsp.	15 mL
Oyster sauce	2 tbsp.	30 mL
Peanut (or cooking) oil	1 tbsp.	15 mL
Green onions, cut into 1 inch (2.5 cm) pieces	3	3
Peanut (or cooking) oil	1 tbsp.	15 mL
Sliced celery	1/2 cup	125 mL
Red pepper slices	1/2 cup	125 mL
Sliced water chestnuts	1/2 cup	125 mL
Thinly sliced carrot	1/3 cup	75 mL
Canned baby corn, drained and cut in half lengthwise	2/3 cup	150 mL
Cashews, toasted (see Tip, page 103)	2/3 cup	150 mL

Marinade: Combine first 6 ingredients in medium bowl.

Add beef. Stir until coated. Marinate at room temperature for 10 minutes.

Stir water into cornstarch in small cup. Add oyster sauce. Stir. Set aside.

Heat wok or large frying pan on medium-high until very hot. Add first amount of peanut oil. Add beef with marinade and green onion. Stir-fry for 3 to 4 minutes until beef reaches desired doneness. Transfer to plate.

Add second amount of peanut oil to wok. Add next 5 ingredients. Stir-fry for 2 to 3 minutes until vegetables are tender-crisp.

(continued on next page)

Main Dishes

Add beef and cashews. Stir cornstarch mixture. Stir into beef mixture for 2 to 3 minutes until boiling and thickened. Makes 3 3/4 cups (925 mL). Serves 4.

1 serving: 415 Calories; 25 g Total Fat (12.4 g Mono, 4.7 g Poly, 5.8 g Sat); 43 mg Cholesterol; 26 g Carbohydrate; 2 g Fibre; 24 g Protein; 1150 mg Sodium

Pictured on front cover.

Beef And Green Peppers

The dark glaze is subtly flavoured with fresh ginger and soy sauce. This has a smaller yield so serve with another meat dish.

Prepared beef broth	1/4 cup	60 mL
Cornstarch	1 tbsp.	15 mL
Soy sauce	2 tbsp.	30 mL
Dry sherry	1 tbsp.	15 mL
Granulated sugar	1/2 tsp.	2 mL
Sirloin steak, cut across grain into 1/8 inch (3 mm) thick slices	3/4 lb.	340 g
Cooking oil	1 tbsp.	15 mL
Finely grated peeled gingerroot	1 tsp.	5 mL
Garlic cloves, minced (or 1/2 tsp., 2 mL, powder)	2	2
Medium green peppers, halved lengthwise and thinly sliced	2	2
Thinly sliced leek (white and tender green parts only) or onion	1/2 cup	125 mL

Stir broth into cornstarch in small cup. Add soy sauce, sherry and sugar. Stir. Set aside.

Cut beef slices into 2 inch (5 cm) strips.

Heat wok or large frying pan on medium-high until very hot. Add cooking oil. Add beef, ginger and garlic. Stir-fry for about 2 minutes until beef is browned.

Add green pepper and leek. Stir-fry for 2 to 3 minutes until tender-crisp. Stir cornstarch mixture. Stir into beef mixture until boiling and thickened. Makes 3 1/2 cups (875 mL). Serves 3 to 4.

1 serving: 294 Calories; 15 g Total Fat (7.1 g Mono, 1.9 g Poly, 4.4 g Sat); 56 mg Cholesterol; 15 g Carbohydrate; 2 g Fibre; 24 g Protein; 834 mg Sodium

Braised Beef Curry

The beef is surrounded by a rich tomato curry sauce with a
wonderful, bold flavour. Spoon the excess sauce over rice or noodles.

MARINADE

Garlic cloves, minced (or 1/2 tsp., 2 mL, powder)	2	2
Dry sherry	2 tbsp.	30 mL
Soy sauce	2 tbsp.	30 mL
Curry paste	1 1/2 tbsp.	25 mL
Sirloin steak, cut across grain into 1/8 inch (3 mm) thick slices	1 lb.	454 g
Cooking oil	2 tbsp.	30 mL
Medium onion, chopped	1	1
Water	1/2 cup	125 mL
Can of stewed tomatoes (with juice)	14 oz.	398 mL
Ketchup	2 tbsp.	30 mL
Granulated sugar	1/2 tsp.	2 mL
Water	2 tbsp.	30 mL
Cornstarch	2 tsp.	10 mL
Green onions, sliced	2	2

Marinade: Combine first 4 ingredients in medium bowl.

Cut beef slices into 2 inch (5 cm) strips. Add to marinade. Stir until coated. Marinate at room temperature for 30 minutes.

Heat wok or large frying pan on medium-high until very hot. Add cooking oil. Add beef and marinade. Stir-fry for 3 to 4 minutes until beef is browned.

Add onion. Stir-fry for about 2 minutes until onion is starting to soften.

Add next 4 ingredients. Bring to a boil. Reduce heat to medium-low. Cover. Simmer for 30 to 40 minutes until beef is tender.

Stir second amount of water into cornstarch in small cup. Stir into beef mixture until boiling and thickened.

Sprinkle with green onion. Makes 4 1/2 cups (1.1 L). Serves 4 to 6.

1 serving: 330 Calories; 18.7 g Total Fat (9.1 g Mono, 2.9 g Poly, 4.6 g Sat); 56 mg Cholesterol; 16 g Carbohydrate; 2 g Fibre; 24 g Protein; 949 mg Sodium

Pictured on page 53.

Beef And Mushrooms

A fragrant and flavourful combination, seasoned with Chinese five-spice powder and ginger. An expensive meat but so very tender.

Chinese dried mushrooms	12	12
Boiling water, to cover		
Water	1 tbsp.	15 mL
Cornstarch	1 tsp.	5 mL
Soy sauce	1 tbsp.	15 mL
Hoisin sauce	1 tbsp.	15 mL
Liquid honey	1 tbsp.	15 mL
Dry sherry	1 tbsp.	15 mL
Pepper	1/4 tsp.	1 mL
Chinese five-spice powder	1/4 tsp.	1 mL
Beef tenderloin	1 lb.	454 g
Cooking oil	2 tsp.	10 mL
Cooking oil	2 tsp.	10 mL
Finely grated peeled gingerroot	1 tsp.	5 mL
Green onions, cut into 1 inch (2.5 cm) pieces	6	6

Put mushrooms into small bowl. Add boiling water. Let stand for 20 minutes until softened. Drain. Remove and discard stems. Slice caps thinly. Set aside.

Stir water into cornstarch in separate small bowl. Add next 6 ingredients. Stir. Set aside.

Remove silver skin from tenderloin. Cut beef in half lengthwise. Cut each half across grain into 1/8 inch (3 mm) thick slices. Heat wok or large frying pan on medium-high until very hot. Add first amount of cooking oil. Stir-fry beef, in 2 batches, for 2 to 3 minutes until browned. Transfer to medium bowl.

Add remaining 3 ingredients to wok. Stir-fry for about 1 minute until fragrant. Add beef and mushrooms. Stir soy sauce mixture. Stir into beef mixture for 2 to 3 minutes until boiling and thickened. Makes about 2 1/2 cups (625 mL). Serves 4.

1 serving: 285 Calories; 12.9 g Total Fat (5.9 g Mono, 1.8 g Poly, 3.4 g Sat); 57 mg Cholesterol; 17 g Carbohydrate; 2 g Fibre; 25 g Protein; 429 mg Sodium

Ginger Beef

This tastes just like your favourite take-out dish! The honey
sweet glaze and the gingery kick will delight everyone!

Water	1/2 cup	125 mL
Cornstarch	1 1/2 tsp.	7 mL
Liquid honey	1/4 cup	60 mL
Oyster sauce	1 1/2 tbsp.	25 mL
Dried crushed chilies	1/2 tsp.	2 mL
Sesame oil	2 tsp.	10 mL
Cornstarch	1/2 cup	125 mL
Large eggs	2	2
Soy sauce	1 tbsp.	15 mL
Sesame oil (optional)	1 tsp.	5 mL
Garlic cloves, minced (or 1/2 tsp., 2 mL, powder)	2	2
Finely grated peeled gingerroot	1 1/2 tsp.	7 mL
Sirloin steak, cut across grain into 1/8 inch (3 mm) thick slices	1 1/4 lbs.	560 g
Cooking oil, for deep-frying		
Cooking oil	2 tsp.	10 mL
Green onions, cut julienne	2	2
Medium carrots, cut julienne	2	2
Finely chopped peeled gingerroot	1 tbsp.	15 mL

Stir water into first amount of cornstarch in small bowl. Add next 4 ingredients. Stir. Set aside.

Beat next 6 ingredients with fork in medium bowl.

Cut beef slices into 1/4 to 1/2 inch (6 to 12 mm) shreds. Add to egg mixture. Stir until coated. Marinate at room temperature for 15 minutes.

Deep-fry beef, in several batches, in hot (375°F, 190°C) cooking oil for 1 to 1 1/2 minutes, stirring and breaking pieces apart, until golden brown. Remove beef with slotted spoon to paper towels to drain. Keep warm.

(continued on next page)

Heat second amount of cooking oil in medium frying pan on medium-high until hot. Add green onion, carrot and second amount of ginger. Stir-fry for about 2 minutes until softened. Stir honey mixture. Stir into carrot mixture until boiling and slightly thickened. Pour over beef. Makes 6 cups (1.5 L). Serves 6.

1 serving: 493 Calories; 31.6 g Total Fat (16.4 g Mono, 7.2 g Poly, 5.5 g Sat); 118 mg Cholesterol; 32 g Carbohydrate; 1 g Fibre; 21 g Protein; 357 mg Sodium

Pictured on page 53.

Chicken With Ginger

Freshly grated ginger is a must for this colourful dish.

Water	1/2 cup	125 mL
Cornstarch	1 tbsp.	15 mL
Soy sauce	1 tbsp.	15 mL
Chicken bouillon powder	2 tsp.	10 mL
Cooking oil	1 tbsp.	15 mL
Boneless, skinless chicken breast halves (about 4), diced	1 lb.	454 g
Finely grated peeled gingerroot	1 tbsp.	15 mL
Sliced fresh white mushrooms	2 cups	500 mL
Slivered green or red pepper	1 1/3 cups	325 mL
Fresh pea pods (or green beans)	1 cup	250 mL
Thinly sliced green onion	2/3 cup	150 mL
Salt	1 tsp.	5 mL
Pepper	1/4 tsp.	1 mL

Stir water into cornstarch in small cup. Add soy sauce and bouillon powder. Stir. Set aside.

Heat wok or large frying pan on medium-high until very hot. Add cooking oil. Add chicken and ginger. Stir-fry for about 3 minutes until chicken is partially cooked.

Add mushrooms, green pepper and pea pods. Stir-fry for 2 to 3 minutes until vegetables are tender-crisp and chicken is no longer pink.

Add green onion, salt and pepper. Stir cornstarch mixture. Stir into chicken mixture until boiling and thickened. Makes 4 cups (1 L).

1 cup (250 mL): 218 Calories; 6 g Total Fat (2.6 g Mono, 1.7 g Poly, 0.9 g Sat); 66 mg Cholesterol; 12 g Carbohydrate; 2 g Fibre; 29 g Protein; 1187 mg Sodium

Diced Chicken And Almonds

An attractive and delicious dish to serve over rice.

Prepared chicken broth	3/4 cup	175 mL
Cornstarch	2 tsp.	10 mL
Soy sauce	1 tbsp.	15 mL
Dry sherry	1 tbsp.	15 mL
Garlic powder	1/4 tsp.	1 mL
Ground ginger	1/4 tsp.	1 mL
Cornstarch	2 tbsp.	30 mL
Egg white (large)	1	1
Salt	1/2 tsp.	2 mL
Boneless, skinless chicken breast halves (about 4), cut into 3/4 inch (2 cm) cubes	1 lb.	454 g
Cooking oil, for deep-frying		
Cooking oil	1 tbsp.	15 mL
Whole almonds (without skin)	1/2 cup	125 mL
Cubed celery, about 1/2 – 3/4 inch (12 – 20 mm) pieces	3/4 cup	175 mL
Quartered fresh brown (or white) mushrooms	3/4 cup	175 mL
Cubed carrot, about 1/2 inch (12 mm) pieces	1/2 cup	125 mL
Chopped canned bamboo shoots	1/2 cup	125 mL
Chopped red pepper, about 1/2 inch (12 mm) pieces	1/2 cup	125 mL
Green onions, cut into 3/4 inch (2 cm) pieces	4	4

Stir broth into first amount of cornstarch in small cup. Add next
4 ingredients. Stir. Set aside.

(continued on next page)

Beat second amount of cornstarch, egg white and salt with fork in medium bowl. Add chicken. Stir until coated.

Deep-fry, 1/3 of chicken pieces at a time, in hot (375°F, 190°C) cooking oil, stirring to separate pieces, for about 5 minutes until golden. Remove to paper towels to drain.

Heat wok or large frying pan on medium until hot. Add second amount of cooking oil. Add almonds. Cook for about 1 minute, stirring constantly, until golden. Remove with slotted spoon to chicken.

Add remaining 6 ingredients to wok. Stir-fry for about 3 minutes until vegetables are tender-crisp. Stir cornstarch mixture. Stir into vegetable mixture for about 3 minutes until boiling and thickened. Add chicken and almonds. Stir for about 1 minute until heated through. Makes 5 cups (1.25 L). Serves 4.

1 serving: 463 Calories; 30.5 g Total Fat (17.7 g Mono, 8 g Poly, 2.9 g Sat); 66 mg Cholesterol; 15 g Carbohydrate; 4 g Fibre; 33 g Protein; 765 mg Sodium

Pictured on page 71.

 To slice meat easily, place in the freezer for about 30 minutes until just beginning to freeze. Or if using from frozen state, only partially thaw. Cut according to recipe instructions.

Almond Chicken

A crunchy dish complemented by tender chunks of chicken.

Ingredient	Imperial	Metric
Water	1/2 cup	125 mL
Cornstarch	2 tsp.	10 mL
Chicken bouillon powder	1 tsp.	5 mL
Cooking oil	1 tbsp.	15 mL
Boneless, skinless chicken breast halves (about 4), cut into 1/2 inch (12 mm) cubes	1 lb.	454 g
Chopped onion	1/4 cup	60 mL
Finely grated peeled gingerroot	1 tsp.	5 mL
Green onions, thinly sliced	2	2
Canned bamboo shoots	1/2 cup	125 mL
Soy sauce	2 tsp.	10 mL
Granulated sugar	1 tsp.	5 mL
Dry sherry	2 tsp.	10 mL
Slivered almonds, toasted (see Tip, page 103)	1 cup	250 mL

Stir water into cornstarch in small cup. Add bouillon powder. Stir. Set aside.

Heat wok or large frying pan on medium-high until very hot. Add cooking oil. Add chicken, onion and ginger. Stir-fry for about 4 minutes until chicken is no longer pink.

Add remaining 6 ingredients. Stir-fry for 1 minute. Stir cornstarch mixture. Stir into chicken mixture until boiling and thickened. Makes 3 cups (750 mL).

1/2 cup (125 mL): 255 Calories; 15.7 g Total Fat (9.5 g Mono, 3.5 g Poly, 1.7 g Sat); 44 mg Cholesterol; 8 g Carbohydrate; 2 g Fibre; 22 g Protein; 228 mg Sodium

1. Diced Chicken And Almonds, page 68
2. Chicken Hot Pot, page 86
3. Chicken And Cashews, page 82
4. Pineapple Chicken, page 74
5. Steamed Rice, page 131

Props Courtesy Of: Chintz & Company
The Bay

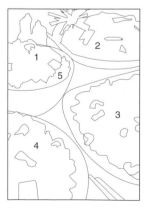

Main Dishes

Chicken Foo Yong

Don't worry if these omelets are irregularly shaped as they usually are in restaurants as well. Serve with Foo Yong Sauce, page 101.

Large eggs, fork-beaten	4	4
Diced cooked chicken	1/2 cup	125 mL
Frozen peas, thawed and drained	1/2 cup	125 mL
Green onions, sliced	2	2
Soy sauce	1 tsp.	5 mL
Salt	1/2 tsp.	2 mL
Dry sherry	2 tsp.	10 mL
Cornstarch	1 tsp.	5 mL
Cooking oil	1 tbsp.	15 mL
Chopped fresh bean sprouts	1 cup	250 mL

Combine first 6 ingredients in medium bowl.

Stir sherry into cornstarch in small cup. Add to chicken mixture. Stir.

Heat large non-stick frying pan on medium until hot. Add cooking oil. Add bean sprouts. Stir-fry for about 30 seconds until almost tender-crisp. Spread out over bottom of frying pan in even layer. Spoon chicken mixture over top. Reduce heat to medium-low. Cover. Cook for 2 minutes. Push cooked egg from outside edge slightly towards centre, allowing uncooked egg to flow down onto pan. Cover. Cook for 2 to 3 minutes until almost set on top. Cut omelet into 4 portions with straight edge on pancake lifter. Turn each portion. Expect edges to look slightly uneven. Cook, uncovered, for about 2 minutes until light brown. Makes 4 portions.

1 portion: 161 Calories; 9 g Total Fat (4.1 g Mono, 1.8 g Poly, 1.9 g Sat); 231 mg Cholesterol; 6 g Carbohydrate; 1 g Fibre; 14 g Protein; 470 mg Sodium

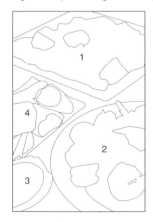

1. Fish In Szechuan Sauce, page 92
2. Five-Spice Shrimp, page 87
3. Sweet And Sour Sauce, page 15
4. Princess Shrimp Rolls, page 21

Props Courtesy Of: Chintz & Company

Pineapple Chicken

Crispy chicken fritters are tossed with juicy pineapple and fresh green peppers, and drizzled with a tangy sauce.

BATTER

All-purpose flour	1 cup	250 mL
Cornstarch	3 tbsp.	50 mL
Salt	3/4 tsp.	4 mL
Large eggs	3	3
Water	4 1/2 tbsp.	67 mL
Boneless, skinless chicken breast halves and/or thighs, cut into 3/4 inch (2 cm) pieces (about 2 cups, 500 mL)	1 lb.	454 g
Cooking oil, for deep-frying		

PINEAPPLE SAUCE

Cooking oil	1 tsp.	5 mL
Coarsely chopped onion	1/3 cup	75 mL
Can of pineapple tidbits (with juice)	14 oz.	398 mL
Brown sugar, packed	1/2 cup	125 mL
Apple cider vinegar	3 tbsp.	50 mL
Salt	1/2 tsp.	2 mL
Unsweetened pineapple juice (or water)	1/2 cup	125 mL
Cornstarch	2 tbsp.	30 mL
Chopped green pepper, cut into 3/4 inch (2 cm) pieces	1/2 cup	125 mL

Batter: Stir flour, cornstarch and salt in medium bowl. Make a well in centre.

Beat eggs and water with fork in small bowl. Add to well. Stir until consistency of medium-thick batter and only few lumps remain.

Add chicken. Stir until coated. Remove, 1 piece at a time with fork or spoon, to hot (375°F, 190°C) cooking oil in deep fryer or wok. Stir with slotted spoon until chicken comes to surface to brown evenly. Deep-fry, in 3 or 4 batches, for about 5 minutes, turning until golden brown on all sides and chicken is no longer pink. Remove to paper towels to drain.

Pineapple Sauce: Heat cooking oil in medium saucepan or wok on medium. Add onion. Cook for 1 to 2 minutes until starting to soften.

(continued on next page)

Add pineapple with juice, brown sugar, vinegar and salt. Bring to a boil.

Stir pineapple juice into cornstarch in small cup. Add to pineapple mixture. Add green pepper. Heat and stir until boiling and thickened. Makes 3 cups (750 mL) sauce. Arrange chicken on platter or in bowl. Pour pineapple sauce over top. Serves 6 to 8.

1 serving: 625 Calories; 33.9 g Total Fat (18.8 g Mono, 9.6 g Poly, 3.3 g Sat); 152 mg Cholesterol; 58 g Carbohydrate; 2 g Fibre; 23 g Protein; 536 mg Sodium

Pictured on page 71.

Sesame Chicken

A visually appealing dish with chunks of chicken and julienned carrots. The sesame sauce has a subtle and delicious flavour.

Prepared chicken broth	1/3 cup	75 mL
Cornstarch	2 tsp.	10 mL
Soy sauce	1 tbsp.	15 mL
Sesame seeds, toasted (see Tip, page 103)	1 tbsp.	15 mL
Brown sugar, packed	2 tsp.	10 mL
Sesame oil	1/2 tsp.	2 mL
Peanut (or cooking) oil	2 tbsp.	30 mL
Boneless chicken thighs, skin removed, cut into 3/4 inch (2 cm) pieces	1 lb.	454 g
Medium carrots, cut julienne	2	2
Medium leeks (white and tender green parts only), halved lengthwise and sliced	2	2
Garlic cloves, minced (or 1/2 tsp., 2 mL, powder)	2	2

Stir broth into cornstarch in small cup. Add next 4 ingredients. Stir. Set aside.

Heat wok or large frying pan on medium-high until very hot. Add peanut oil. Add chicken. Stir-fry for about 4 minutes until no longer pink. Remove with slotted spoon to plate, leaving any excess peanut oil in wok.

Add carrot, leek and garlic. Stir-fry for 2 to 3 minutes until starting to soften. Add chicken. Stir cornstarch mixture. Stir into chicken mixture for 1 to 2 minutes until boiling and thickened. Makes 4 cups (1 L). Serves 4.

1 serving: 300 Calories; 14.5 g Total Fat (5.6 g Mono, 4.4 g Poly, 3 g Sat); 94 mg Cholesterol; 18 g Carbohydrate; 3 g Fibre; 24 g Protein; 358 mg Sodium

Lemon Chicken

This is always a favourite dish in Chinese restaurants. These tender strips of chicken present beautifully on a bed of shredded lettuce. Drizzle with this savoury sauce and garnish with lemon slices. Delicious!

Water	1/4 cup	60 mL
Large eggs	2	2
Cornstarch	1/2 cup	125 mL
Salt	1/2 tsp.	2 mL
White (or black) pepper	1/8 tsp.	0.5 mL
Boneless, skinless chicken breast halves (about 1 lb., 454 g)	4	4
Cooking oil, for deep-frying	4 cups	1 L
LEMON SAUCE		
Prepared chicken broth	1 cup	250 mL
Granulated sugar	1/4 cup	60 mL
Cornstarch	4 tsp.	20 mL
Ground ginger	1/4 tsp.	1 mL
Salt	1/4 tsp.	1 mL
Lemon curd (or spread)	1/4 cup	60 mL
Lemon juice	3 tbsp.	50 mL
Finely shredded lettuce (or cabbage), optional	2 cups	500 mL
Thinly sliced lemon	1/4 cup	60 mL

Beat water and eggs with fork in medium bowl until frothy. Stir in cornstarch, salt and pepper until smooth.

Pound chicken to 1/4 inch (6 mm) thickness. Blot dry with paper towel. Coat with batter.

Deep-fry, 2 at a time, in hot (375°F, 190°C) cooking oil for 1 1/2 to 2 minutes per side until golden and no longer pink inside. Remove to paper towels to drain. Keep warm.

Lemon Sauce: Stir broth, sugar, cornstarch, ginger and salt in small saucepan. Heat on medium for about 5 minutes, stirring constantly, until boiling and thickened.

Stir in lemon curd and lemon juice until smooth and bubbling. Makes 1 1/3 cups (325 mL) sauce.

(continued on next page)

Main Dishes

Arrange lettuce and lemon slices on small platter. Slice chicken crosswise at angle into 4 or 5 pieces each. Arrange over lettuce. Pour lemon sauce over top. Serves 4.

1 serving: 502 Calories; 23.2 g Total Fat (11.8 g Mono, 5.9 g Poly, 3.5 g Sat); 201 mg Cholesterol; 42 g Carbohydrate; trace Fibre; 31 g Protein; 853 mg Sodium

Pictured on page 18 and on back cover.

Old Country Chicken

When my friends, the Eng family, came to Canada, this is one of the many recipes that came with them. This is sure to become one of your favourites too!

SAUCE

Ketchup	1 cup	250 mL
Smooth peanut butter	1 tsp.	5 mL
Hoisin sauce	1 cup	250 mL
Vietnamese hot pepper sauce	2 – 3 tbsp.	30 – 50 mL
Brown sugar, packed	2 tbsp.	30 mL
Sesame oil	2 tsp.	10 mL
Garlic cloves, finely diced (or 1 tsp., 5 mL, powder)	4	4
Chicken drumsticks and thighs (about 12 pieces), skin removed	3 lbs.	1.4 kg

Sauce: Combine ketchup and peanut butter in small bowl until well blended.

Add next 5 ingredients. Mix well. Makes 2 1/2 cups (625 mL) sauce. Transfer 1/2 of sauce to small saucepan. Bring to a boil on medium. Reduce heat to medium-low. Simmer, uncovered, for about 10 minutes, stirring frequently, until slightly reduced. Serve warm as dipping sauce for chicken. Makes about 1 cup (250 mL).

Coat chicken generously with remaining 1/2 of sauce. Arrange on greased foil-lined baking sheet. Place oven rack on second from top position. Broil, watching carefully, until a few black spots appear on sauce. Turn off broiler. Turn oven to 400°F (205°C). Bake chicken for about 45 minutes until tender and no longer pink inside. Makes about 12 pieces. Serves 6.

1 serving: 548 Calories; 17.7 g Total Fat (6.3 g Mono, 4.6 g Poly, 4.5 g Sat); 191 mg Cholesterol; 44 g Carbohydrate; 2 g Fibre; 52 g Protein; 1583 mg Sodium

Moo Goo Gai Pan

A flavourful and attractive dish. Serve with fried rice or noodles.

Prepared chicken broth	1/4 cup	60 mL
Cornstarch	2 tsp.	10 mL
Dry sherry	2 tbsp.	30 mL
Salt	1/2 tsp.	2 mL
Garlic powder (optional)	1/4 tsp.	1 mL
Soy sauce	1 tbsp.	15 mL
Sesame oil	1 tsp.	5 mL
Finely grated peeled gingerroot	1/2 tsp.	2 mL
Boneless, skinless chicken breast halves (about 3), sliced 1/4 inch (6 mm) thick and cut julienne	12 oz.	340 g
Cooking oil	1 tbsp.	15 mL
Cooking oil	1 tbsp.	15 mL
Suey choy (Chinese cabbage), shredded	1 cup	250 mL
Thinly sliced celery	1/2 cup	125 mL
Fresh pea pods, cut julienne	1/2 cup	125 mL
Fresh shiitake mushrooms, stems removed and discarded, caps sliced (or sliced brown mushrooms)	1 cup	250 mL
Canned bamboo shoots, cut julienne	1/4 cup	60 mL
Sesame seeds, toasted (see Tip, page 103), for garnish	1 tsp.	5 mL

Stir broth into cornstarch in small bowl. Add next 3 ingredients. Stir. Set aside.

Combine soy sauce, sesame oil and ginger in medium bowl. Add chicken. Stir until coated. Cover. Marinate at room temperature for 15 minutes.

Heat wok or large frying pan on medium-high until very hot. Add first amount of cooking oil. Add chicken and marinade. Stir-fry for 2 to 3 minutes until chicken is no longer pink. Transfer to bowl. Keep warm.

Heat second amount of cooking oil in wok. Add next 5 ingredients. Stir-fry for about 2 minutes until vegetables are tender-crisp. Stir broth mixture. Stir into vegetable mixture for about 1 minute until boiling and thickened. Add chicken. Stir until heated through.

(continued on next page)

Main Dishes

Sprinkle with sesame seeds. Makes 4 cups (1 L). Serves 4.

1 serving: 223 Calories; 10.2 g Total Fat (5.1 g Mono, 3.1 g Poly, 1.2 g Sat); 49 mg Cholesterol; 10 g Carbohydrate; 2 g Fibre; 22 g Protein; 629 mg Sodium

Pictured on page 54.

Satay Chicken

This delicious dish is coated in a thick, creamy sauce. Buy the satay sauce that comes in a jar and resembles a paste. If you're short on time this is a great dish to throw together. It's so easy to make!

Prepared chicken broth	1/4 cup	60 mL
Cornstarch	2 tsp.	10 mL
Peanut (or cooking) oil	1 tbsp.	15 mL
Boneless chicken thighs, skin removed, sliced	1 1/2 lbs.	680 g
Peanut (or cooking) oil	2 tsp.	10 mL
Medium onion, cut into 16 wedges	1	1
Garlic clove, minced (or 1/4 tsp., 1 mL, powder)	1	1
Chinese satay sauce	1/2 cup	125 mL
Green onion, thinly sliced	1	1

Stir broth into cornstarch in small cup. Set aside.

Heat wok or large frying pan on medium-high until very hot. Add first amount of peanut oil. Stir-fry chicken, in 2 batches, for 3 to 4 minutes until browned. Transfer to medium bowl.

Heat second amount of peanut oil in wok. Add onion and garlic. Stir-fry for 2 to 3 minutes until onion is tender-crisp.

Add chicken and satay sauce. Stir-fry for about 1 minute until chicken is no longer pink. Stir cornstarch mixture. Stir into chicken mixture until boiling and thickened.

Sprinkle with green onion. Makes 4 cups (1 L).

1 cup (250 mL): 410 Calories; 25 g Total Fat (9.6 g Mono, 6.4 g Poly, 6.5 g Sat); 141 mg Cholesterol; 8 g Carbohydrate; 1 g Fibre; 38 g Protein; 652 mg Sodium

Kung Pao Chicken

A dish known for its spicy kick. Serve over rice or noodles.

Prepared chicken broth	2/3 cup	150 mL
Cornstarch	1 1/2 tbsp.	25 mL
Soy sauce	2 tbsp.	30 mL
Hoisin sauce	2 tbsp.	30 mL
Dry sherry	2 tbsp.	30 mL
Chili paste (sambal oelek)	2 tsp.	10 mL
Egg white (large)	1	1
Cornstarch	1 tbsp.	15 mL
Sesame oil	1 tsp.	5 mL
Boneless, skinless chicken breast halves (about 4), cut into 3/4 inch (2 cm) cubes	1 lb.	454 g
Cooking oil, for deep-frying		
Cooking oil	1 tbsp.	15 mL
Cubed red, yellow and/or green peppers, cut into 3/4 inch (2 cm) pieces	1 1/2 cups	375 mL
Diced carrot	1/2 cup	125 mL
Diced celery	1/2 cup	125 mL
Diced onion	1/2 cup	125 mL
Garlic cloves, minced (or 1/2 tsp., 2 mL, powder)	2	2
Finely grated peeled gingerroot	1 tsp.	5 mL
Green onions, cut into 1 inch (2.5 cm) pieces	2	2
Roasted peanuts, coarsely chopped	1/2 cup	125 mL

Stir broth into cornstarch in small bowl. Add next 4 ingredients. Stir. Set aside.

Beat next 3 ingredients with fork in medium bowl. Add chicken. Stir until coated.

Deep-fry, in 2 batches, in hot (375°F, 190°C) cooking oil for 3 to 4 minutes, stirring to separate pieces, until golden brown. Remove with slotted spoon to paper towels to drain. Keep warm.

Heat wok or large frying pan on medium-high until very hot. Add second amount of cooking oil. Add next 7 ingredients. Stir-fry for 3 to 4 minutes until tender-crisp. Stir broth mixture. Stir into vegetable mixture for about 30 seconds until boiling and thickened. Add chicken. Stir until coated with sauce and heat through.

(continued on next page)

Sprinkle with peanuts. Makes 6 cups (1.5 L). Serves 4 to 6.

1 serving: 511 Calories; 31.2 g Total Fat (16.4 g Mono, 9.5 g Poly, 3.4 g Sat); 66 mg Cholesterol; 24 g Carbohydrate; 4 g Fibre; 34 g Protein; 907 mg Sodium

Pictured on page 54.

Coconut Chicken

This dish has a wonderful taste and texture combination.

Whole bone-in chicken breast halves (with skin)	2	2
Medium coconut	1/3 cup	75 mL
Water	2 cups	500 mL
Chicken bouillon powder	1 tsp.	5 mL
Water	2 tbsp.	30 mL
Cornstarch	4 tsp.	20 mL
Salt	1/2 tsp.	2 mL
Pepper	1/8 tsp.	0.5 mL
Cooking oil	1 tbsp.	15 mL
Chopped celery	1 cup	250 mL
Water chestnuts, chopped	4	4
Chopped baby bok choy (or spinach), lightly packed	1 cup	250 mL

Cut chicken away from bones. Put bones and skin into large saucepan. Cut meat into 1/2 inch (12 mm) cubes. You should have about 1 1/4 cups (300 mL). Set aside.

Add coconut, first amount of water and bouillon powder to bones. Bring to a boil. Cover. Boil for 30 minutes. Tip saucepan so fat comes to top. Spoon off as much fat as you can. Strain liquid into large bowl. Discard solids.

Stir second amount of water into cornstarch in small cup. Add salt and pepper. Stir. Set aside.

Heat wok or large frying pan on medium-high until very hot. Add cooking oil. Add celery and chicken. Stir-fry for 1 to 2 minutes until chicken is no longer pink. Add strained liquid. Bring to a boil.

Add water chestnuts and bok choy. Cook, uncovered, for about 2 minutes until bok choy wilts. Stir cornstarch mixture. Stir into chicken mixture until boiling and thickened. Makes 3 cups (750 mL).

1 cup (250 mL): 396 Calories; 14.9 g Total Fat (3.9 g Mono, 2.3 g Poly, 7.3 g Sat); 109 mg Cholesterol; 20 g Carbohydrate; 3 g Fibre; 44 g Protein; 676 mg Sodium

Chicken And Cashews

Vegetables, chicken and nuts in a slightly sweet sauce.

Chinese dried mushrooms	8	8
Boiling water, to cover		
Prepared chicken broth	1/4 cup	60 mL
Cornstarch	1 tbsp.	15 mL
Soy sauce	2 tbsp.	30 mL
Liquid honey	1 tbsp.	15 mL
Oyster sauce	1 tbsp.	15 mL
Peanut (or cooking) oil	1 tbsp.	15 mL
Boneless chicken thighs, skin removed, cut into 3/4 inch (2 cm) pieces	1 lb.	454 g
Peanut (or cooking) oil	1 tbsp.	15 mL
Garlic cloves, minced (or 1/2 tsp., 2 mL, powder)	2	2
Finely grated peeled gingerroot	1 tsp.	5 mL
Chopped Shanghai bok choy	3 cups	750 mL
Green onions, cut into 1 inch (2.5 cm) pieces	6	6
Cashews, toasted (see Tip, page 103)	2/3 cup	150 mL

Put mushrooms into small bowl. Add boiling water. Let stand for 20 minutes until softened. Drain. Remove and discard stems. Cut caps in half.

Stir broth into cornstarch in small cup. Add next 3 ingredients. Stir. Set aside.

Heat wok or large frying pan on medium-high until very hot. Add first amount of peanut oil. Stir-fry chicken, in 2 batches, for 3 to 4 minutes until browned. Transfer to medium bowl.

Heat second amount of peanut oil in wok. Add garlic and ginger. Stir-fry for about 1 minute until fragrant.

Add bok choy and green onion. Add chicken and mushrooms. Stir cornstarch mixture. Stir into chicken mixture until chicken is tender and bok choy is tender-crisp.

Add cashews. Stir-fry for about 1 minute until well combined and hot. Makes 5 cups (1.25 L).

1 cup (250 mL): 287 Calories; 17.7 g Total Fat (8.8 g Mono, 4.1 g Poly, 3.5 g Sat); 45 mg Cholesterol; 19 g Carbohydrate; 2 g Fibre; 16 g Protein; 790 mg Sodium

Pictured on page 71.

Braised Chicken And Noodles

The taste of Chinese five-spice powder is evident in this warm, savoury dish.

Medium rice stick noodles	4 oz.	113 g
Boiling water, to cover		
Chinese dried mushrooms	8	8
Boiling water, to cover		
Prepared chicken broth	1/3 cup	75 mL
Soy sauce	2 tbsp.	30 mL
Chinese barbecue sauce	1 tbsp.	15 mL
Liquid honey	1 tbsp.	15 mL
Chinese five-spice powder (optional)	1/4 tsp.	1 mL
Cooking oil	1 tbsp.	15 mL
Boneless chicken thighs, skin removed, quartered	1 1/2 lbs.	680 g
Cooking oil	2 tsp.	10 mL
Finely grated peeled gingerroot	1 tsp.	5 mL
Garlic clove, minced (or 1/4 tsp., 1 mL, powder)	1	1

Put noodles into large bowl. Add boiling water. Let stand for 20 minutes until softened. Drain. Rinse under cold water. Drain well. Set aside.

Put mushrooms into small bowl. Add boiling water. Let stand for 20 minutes until softened. Drain. Remove and discard stems. Slice caps. Set aside.

Combine next 5 ingredients in separate small bowl.

Heat wok or large frying pan on medium-high until very hot. Add first amount of cooking oil. Stir-fry chicken, in 2 batches, for about 5 minutes until browned. Transfer to medium bowl.

Heat second amount of cooking oil in wok. Add ginger and garlic. Stir-fry for about 1 minute until fragrant. Reduce heat to medium-low. Add chicken. Stir broth mixture. Stir into chicken mixture. Cover. Cook for about 20 minutes until chicken is tender. Add noodles and mushrooms. Stir-fry on medium-high for about 2 minutes until noodles are hot. Makes about 3 1/2 cups (875 mL). Serves 4.

1 serving: 437 Calories; 15.5 g Total Fat (6.3 g Mono, 4.1 g Poly, 2.8 g Sat); 141 mg Cholesterol; 37 g Carbohydrate; 2 g Fibre; 37 g Protein; 627 mg Sodium

Bird's Nest Chicken

A crispy, golden Potato Nest holds this fresh, colourful stir-fry.

Water	1/2 cup	125 mL
Cornstarch	2 tsp.	10 mL
Oyster sauce	2 tbsp.	30 mL
Dry sherry	1 tbsp.	15 mL
Granulated sugar	2 tsp.	10 mL
Dry sherry	2 tsp.	10 mL
Sesame oil	1/2 tsp.	2 mL
Boneless, skinless chicken breast halves (about 2), cut crosswise into 1/8 inch (3 mm) slices	8 oz.	225 g
Cooking oil	1 tbsp.	15 mL
Baby carrots, thinly sliced	2	2
Finely grated peeled gingerroot	1/2 tsp.	2 mL
Small onion, cut into narrow wedges	1	1
Green onions, cut into 2 inch (5 cm) pieces	2	2
Fresh small mushrooms, halved	6	6
Fresh pea pods	10	10
Sliced water chestnuts, rinsed and drained	1/3 cup	75 mL
Canned bamboo shoots, cut julienne	1/3 cup	75 mL
Cooking oil	1 tbsp.	15 mL
Potato Nest (7 inch, 18 cm, size), page 119, warmed	1	1
Julienned cucumber, for garnish		

Stir water into cornstarch in small cup. Add next 3 ingredients. Stir. Set aside.

Combine second amount of sherry and sesame oil in small bowl. Add chicken. Stir until coated. Let stand at room temperature for 5 minutes.

Heat wok or large frying pan on medium-high until very hot. Add first amount of cooking oil. Add next 8 ingredients, in order given, while stir-frying. Stir-fry for about 4 minutes until carrot is tender-crisp. Transfer to medium bowl.

Add second amount of cooking oil to wok. Add chicken and marinade. Stir-fry for about 3 minutes until chicken is starting to brown and no longer pink inside. Add vegetables and any accumulated liquid. Stir cornstarch mixture. Stir into chicken mixture for about 1 minute until boiling and thickened. Makes 2 2/3 cups (650 mL).

(continued on next page)

Main Dishes

Spoon into warm potato nest to serve. Garnish with cucumber. Serves 3 to 4.

1 serving: 456 Calories; 21 g Total Fat (11.5 g Mono, 6.3 g Poly, 1.8 g Sat); 44 mg Cholesterol; 45 g Carbohydrate; 3 g Fibre; 21 g Protein; 680 mg Sodium

Pictured on page 125.

Black Pepper Chicken

Tender chicken and crisp vegetables in this saucy dish.

Prepared chicken broth	1/4 cup	60 mL
Cornstarch	1 tbsp.	15 mL
Soy sauce	2 tbsp.	30 mL
Hoisin sauce	2 tbsp.	30 mL
Liquid honey	1 tbsp.	15 mL
Cooking oil	1 tbsp.	15 mL
Boneless chicken thighs, skin removed, cut into 3/4 inch (2 cm) pieces	1 lb.	454 g
Cooking oil	1 tbsp.	15 mL
Medium onion, cut into 16 wedges	1	1
Garlic cloves, minced (or 1/2 tsp., 2 mL, powder)	2	2
Finely grated peeled gingerroot	1 tsp.	5 mL
Pepper	1 tsp.	5 mL
Can of baby corn, drained and halved	14 oz.	398 mL
Chopped baby bok choy	3 cups	750 mL
Green onions, cut into 1 inch (2.5 cm) pieces	6	6

Stir broth into cornstarch in small bowl. Add next 3 ingredients. Stir. Set aside.

Heat wok or large frying pan on medium-high until very hot. Add first amount of cooking oil. Add chicken. Stir-fry for about 5 minutes until browned. Transfer to medium bowl.

Heat second amount of cooking oil in wok. Add next 4 ingredients. Stir-fry for about 1 minute until fragrant.

Add remaining 3 ingredients. Stir-fry for about 2 minutes until bok choy leaves are wilted. Add chicken. Stir cornstarch mixture. Stir into chicken mixture for about 2 minutes until chicken is tender and bok choy stems are tender-crisp. Makes 6 cups (1.5 L).

1 cup (250 mL): 220 Calories; 9.1 g Total Fat (4.1 g Mono, 2.6 g Poly, 1.4 g Sat); 63 mg Cholesterol; 18 g Carbohydrate; 2 g Fibre; 17 g Protein; 628 mg Sodium

Chicken Hot Pot

The mild Asian flavours in this dish are sure to be a hit!
Perfect served over noodles or rice to soak up the delicious gravy.

Chinese dried mushrooms	12	12
Boiling water, to cover		
Cornstarch	1/4 cup	60 mL
Salt	1/2 tsp.	2 mL
Bone-in chicken thighs (about 2 lbs., 900 g), skin removed	8	8
Peanut (or cooking) oil	1 1/2 tbsp.	25 mL
Cooking oil	1 tbsp.	15 mL
Garlic cloves, minced (or 1/2 tsp., 2 mL, powder)	2	2
Finely grated peeled gingerroot	1/2 tsp.	2 mL
Dry white (or alcohol-free) wine	1/2 cup	125 mL
Prepared chicken broth	1/2 cup	125 mL
Hoisin sauce	2 tbsp.	30 mL
Water	1 tbsp.	15 mL
Cornstarch	2 tsp.	10 mL
Green onions, cut into 1 inch (2.5 cm) pieces	6	6

Put mushrooms into small bowl. Add boiling water. Let stand for 20 minutes until softened. Drain. Remove and discard stems. Cut caps in half. Set aside.

Combine first amount of cornstarch and salt in large resealable freezer bag or shallow dish. Add chicken. Toss until coated.

Heat wok or large frying pan on medium-high until very hot. Add peanut oil. Stir-fry chicken, in 2 batches, until browned. Transfer to medium bowl.

Add cooking oil, garlic and ginger to wok. Stir-fry for about 1 minute until fragrant.

Add mushrooms and next 3 ingredients. Stir. Add chicken. Reduce heat to medium-low. Cover. Simmer for 25 to 30 minutes, stirring occasionally, until chicken is tender.

(continued on next page)

Main Dishes

Stir water into second amount of cornstarch in small cup. Add to chicken mixture. Heat and stir on medium-high until boiling and thickened.

Add green onion. Stir-fry for about 1 minute until bright green. Serves 4 to 6.

1 serving: 361 Calories; 15.7 g Total Fat (6.6 g Mono, 4.4 g Poly, 2.9 g Sat); 103 mg Cholesterol; 24 g Carbohydrate; 2 g Fibre; 26 g Protein; 606 mg Sodium

Pictured on page 71.

Five-Spice Shrimp

Pretty pink shrimp sprinkled with green onion for a very attractive presentation. Adjust the amount of chilies to suit your tastes. Easy to make.

Raw large shrimp (tails intact), peeled and deveined	1 lb.	454 g
Garlic cloves, minced (or 1/2 tsp., 2 mL, powder)	2	2
Dried crushed chilies	1/2 tsp.	2 mL
Salt	1/2 tsp.	2 mL
Pepper	1/4 tsp.	1 mL
Chinese five-spice powder	1/4 tsp.	1 mL
Peanut (or cooking) oil	1 tbsp.	15 mL
Green onion, thinly sliced	1	1

Cut shrimp down back almost, but not quite through, to other side. Press to flatten slightly.

Combine next 5 ingredients in large bowl. Add shrimp. Mix well.

Heat wok or large frying pan on medium-high until very hot. Add peanut oil and shrimp mixture. Stir-fry for 2 to 3 minutes until shrimp are pink.

Sprinkle with green onion. Makes about 2 cups (500 mL). Serves 4.

1 serving: 125 Calories; 5 g Total Fat (1.8 g Mono, 1.7 g Poly, 0.9 g Sat); 129 mg Cholesterol; 2 g Carbohydrate; trace Fibre; 17 g Protein; 427 mg Sodium

Pictured on page 72.

Satay Shrimp

The concentrated satay sauce that comes in a jar and looks like a paste is the secret ingredient in this dish. Its unique flavour adds to the spicy kick in the marinade.

MARINADE

Chinese satay sauce	3 tbsp.	50 mL
Soy sauce	2 tbsp.	30 mL
Liquid honey	1 tbsp.	15 mL
Dry sherry	1 tbsp.	15 mL
Curry powder	1 tsp.	5 mL
Chinese five-spice powder	1/4 tsp.	1 mL
Salt	1/4 tsp.	1 mL
Raw large shrimp, peeled and deveined	2 lbs.	900 g
Cooking oil	1 tbsp.	15 mL
Medium onion, cut into 16 wedges	1	1

Marinade: Combine first 7 ingredients in medium bowl.

Cut shrimp down back almost, but not quite through, to other side. Press to flatten slightly. Add to marinade. Toss until coated. Cover. Marinate in refrigerator for 1 to 3 hours.

Heat wok or large frying pan on medium-high until very hot. Add cooking oil and onion. Stir-fry for about 4 minutes until onion is starting to soften and turn golden brown. Add shrimp and marinade. Stir-fry for about 3 minutes until shrimp are pink. Makes 5 cups (1.25 L). Serves 4.

1 serving: 274 Calories; 8.6 g Total Fat (3.5 g Mono, 2.7 g Poly, 1.2 g Sat); 257 mg Cholesterol; 11 g Carbohydrate; 1 g Fibre; 37 g Protein; 1202 mg Sodium

1. Two-Colour Vegetables, page 137
2. Diced Tofu And Noodles, page 116
3. Oyster Sauce Beef, page 59

Props Courtesy Of: Chintz & Company
Pier 1 Imports

Main Dishes

Shrimp And Scallops

A light, fresh-tasting dish with well-balanced flavours. So quick and easy to make!

Prepared chicken broth	1/4 cup	60 mL
Cornstarch	1 tsp.	5 mL
Oyster sauce	2 tbsp.	30 mL
Sweet soy sauce	1 tbsp.	15 mL
Granulated sugar	1 tsp.	5 mL
Finely grated peeled gingerroot	1/2 tsp.	2 mL
Pepper	1/8 tsp.	0.5 mL
Peanut (or cooking) oil	1 tbsp.	15 mL
Green onions, cut into 1 inch (2.5 cm) pieces	6	6
Garlic clove, minced (or 1/4 tsp., 1 mL, powder)	1	1
Raw large shrimp, peeled and deveined	1 lb.	454 g
Raw large scallops, halved	4 oz.	113 g
Fresh pea pods	1 cup	250 mL

Stir broth into cornstarch in small bowl. Add next 5 ingredients. Stir. Set aside.

Heat wok or large frying pan on medium-high until very hot. Add peanut oil. Add remaining 5 ingredients. Stir-fry for 1 to 2 minutes until shrimp are just starting to turn pink. Stir cornstarch mixture. Stir into shrimp mixture for 1 to 2 minutes until shrimp are pink and pea pods are tender crisp. Makes 4 cups (1 L). Serves 4.

1 serving: 182 Calories; 5.4 g Total Fat (1.9 g Mono, 1.8 g Poly, 1 g Sat); 139 mg Cholesterol; 9 g Carbohydrate; 1 g Fibre; 24 g Protein; 1090 mg Sodium

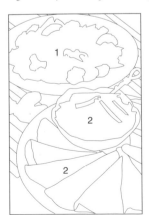

1. Chinese Stir-Fry Vegetables, page 139
2. Moo Shu Pork And Pancakes, page 110

Props Courtesy Of: Chintz & Company
The Bay

Fish In Szechuan Sauce

The fiery hot Szechuan sauce complements the battered white fish.
A delicious dish that is sure to become a favourite!

Prepared chicken broth	1/2 cup	125 mL
Cornstarch	2 tsp.	10 mL
Sweet (or regular) chili sauce	1 tbsp.	15 mL
Rice vinegar	2 tsp.	10 mL
Granulated sugar	1 tsp.	5 mL
Egg white (large)	1	1
Cornstarch	1 tbsp.	15 mL
Firm white fish fillets (or steaks), such as halibut, haddock or sea bass, skin removed, cut into 1 1/2 inch (3.8 cm) cubes	1 1/2 lbs.	680 g
Cooking oil, for deep-frying		
Cooking oil	1 tbsp.	15 mL
Medium onion, halved lengthwise and thinly sliced	1	1
Finely chopped peeled gingerroot	1 tbsp.	15 mL
Garlic clove, minced (or 1/4 tsp., 1 mL, powder)	1	1
Chili black bean sauce	1 – 2 tbsp.	15 – 30 mL
Dry sherry	2 tbsp.	30 mL
Soy sauce	1 tbsp.	15 mL
Green onions, sliced, for garnish	2	2

Stir broth into first amount of cornstarch in small cup. Add next 3 ingredients. Stir. Set aside.

Beat egg white and second amount of cornstarch with fork in medium bowl. Add fish. Stir until coated.

Deep-fry, in 2 batches, in hot (375°F, 190°C) cooking oil for about 4 minutes, stirring to separate fish, until golden brown. Remove with slotted spoon to paper towels to drain. Keep warm.

Heat wok or large frying pan on medium-high until very hot. Add second amount of cooking oil. Add sliced onion, ginger and garlic. Stir-fry for 1 to 2 minutes until fragrant and slightly softened.

(continued on next page)

Main Dishes

Add next 3 ingredients. Stir to blend flavours. Stir cornstarch mixture. Stir into bean sauce mixture for about 30 seconds until boiling and thickened. Add fish. Stir gently until coated with sauce.

Sprinkle with green onion. Serves 6.

1 serving: 348 Calories; 23.7 g Total Fat (13.2 g Mono, 7.2 g Poly, 1.9 g Sat); 36 mg Cholesterol; 7 g Carbohydrate; 1 g Fibre; 25 g Protein; 457 mg Sodium

Pictured on page 72.

Crab Foo Yong

An intense crab flavour dominates this egg dish.
Drizzle with Foo Yong Sauce, page 101.

Large eggs	6	6
Water	2 tbsp.	30 mL
Soy sauce	1 tsp.	5 mL
Salt	1/2 tsp.	2 mL
Can of crabmeat, drained and cartilage removed, flaked (or 1 cup, 250 mL, fresh)	4 1/4 oz.	120 g
Dry sherry	1 tsp.	5 mL
Cooking oil	1 tbsp.	15 mL
Fresh bean sprouts, chopped once or twice	2 cups	500 mL
Green onions, sliced	2	2

Beat eggs, water, soy sauce and salt in small bowl until smooth.

Stir in crab and sherry.

Heat cooking oil in large non-stick frying pan on medium. Add bean sprouts and green onion. Cook for about 1 minute until bean sprouts are barely tender-crisp. Arrange evenly in bottom of frying pan. Reduce heat to medium-low. Carefully pour crab mixture over bean sprouts. Cook, uncovered, for about 7 minutes, pushing edges slightly in towards centre to allow uncooked egg to flow onto pan, until lightly browned on bottom. Cut with pancake lifter into 6 wedges. Turn each wedge. Cook for about 2 minutes until browned. Serves 6.

1 serving: 121 Calories; 7.5 g Total Fat (3.3 g Mono, 1.4 g Poly, 1.7 g Sat); 216 mg Cholesterol; 3 g Carbohydrate; trace Fibre; 10 g Protein; 451 mg Sodium

Pineapple Shrimp

You'll love these succulent, lightly battered shrimp.
The tangy sauce is perfect for dipping or served over the shrimp.

PINEAPPLE SAUCE

Can of pineapple tidbits (or chunks, halved), with juice	14 oz.	398 mL
White vinegar	1/4 cup	60 mL
Brown sugar, packed	1/4 cup	60 mL
Soy sauce	1 tbsp.	15 mL
Medium green pepper, cut into chunks	1	1
Water	1/4 cup	60 mL
Cornstarch	2 tbsp.	30 mL

BATTER

Large eggs	3	3
All-purpose flour	1/2 cup	125 mL
Salt	1 1/2 tsp.	7 mL
Raw medium shrimp, peeled and deveined, blotted dry	1 lb.	454 g
Cooking oil, for deep-frying		

Pineapple Sauce: Combine first 5 ingredients in small saucepan. Bring to a boil.

Stir water into cornstarch in small cup. Stir into pineapple mixture until boiling and thickened. Keep warm. Makes 3 cups (750 mL) sauce.

Batter: Beat eggs in small bowl. Stir in flour and salt.

Dip shrimp into batter. Deep-fry, in batches, in hot (375°F, 190°C) cooking oil for about 4 minutes, turning once, until browned. Remove to paper towels to drain. Keep warm in 200°F (95°C) oven while deep-frying remaining shrimp. Pour sauce over shrimp or serve sauce on side. Serves 4.

1 serving: 484 Calories; 20.1 g Total Fat (10.2 g Mono, 5.5 g Poly, 2.5 g Sat); 291 mg Cholesterol; 52 g Carbohydrate; 2 g Fibre; 25 g Protein; 1333 mg Sodium

Seafood In Black Bean Sauce

Perfectly cooked shrimp and scallops combine with bright,
saucy vegetables in this tasty dish. Serve over rice or with noodles.

Cornstarch	1 tbsp.	15 mL
Water	2 tbsp.	30 mL
Prepared black bean sauce	2/3 cup	150 mL
Dry sherry	2 tbsp.	30 mL
Cooking oil	1 tbsp.	15 mL
Medium onion, cut lengthwise into thin wedges	1	1
Slivered green pepper	1/2 cup	125 mL
Garlic clove, minced (or 1/4 tsp., 1 mL, powder)	1	1
Finely grated peeled gingerroot	1/2 tsp.	2 mL
Cooking oil	1 tbsp.	15 mL
Raw medium shrimp, peeled and deveined	12 oz.	340 g
Raw bay (small) scallops	8 oz.	225 g
Finely shredded suey choy (Chinese cabbage)	1 cup	250 mL
Green onion, thinly sliced	1	1

Stir cornstarch into water in small bowl. Add black bean sauce and sherry. Stir. Set aside.

Heat wok or large frying pan on medium-high until very hot. Add first amount of cooking oil. Add onion, green pepper, garlic and ginger. Stir-fry for about 2 minutes until almost tender-crisp. Transfer to small bowl. Keep warm.

Heat second amount of cooking oil in wok. Add shrimp and scallops. Stir-fry for about 1 minute until shrimp are starting to turn pink and scallops are turning opaque. Do not overcook. Add vegetable mixture. Stir cornstarch mixture. Stir into seafood mixture for about 2 minutes until boiling and thickened. Makes 3 1/2 cups (875 mL).

Arrange suey choy on plate. Spoon seafood mixture over top. Sprinkle with green onion. Serves 6.

1 serving: 188 Calories; 7.9 g Total Fat (4.1 g Mono, 2.4 g Poly, 0.7 g Sat); 77 mg Cholesterol;
11 g Carbohydrate; 2 g Fibre; 17 g Protein; 1225 mg Sodium

Mandarin Whole Fried Fish

These delicate, moist fish are coated in a sweet ginger sauce.
I prefer head off in the kitchen.

MARINADE

Finely grated peeled gingerroot	1 tsp.	5 mL
Onion salt	1 tsp.	5 mL
Pepper, sprinkle		
Dry sherry	1/2 cup	125 mL
Whole rainbow trout (or your choice), pan ready (1/2 – 3/4 lb., 225 – 340 g, each)	2	2
Cornstarch	1/4 cup	60 mL
Cooking oil	2 cups	500 mL
Prepared chicken broth	1/2 cup	125 mL
Cornstarch	2 tsp.	10 mL
Sweet (or regular) chili sauce	2 tbsp.	30 mL
Water	1 tbsp.	15 mL
Sesame oil	2 tsp.	10 mL
Garlic clove, minced (or 1/4 tsp., 1 mL, powder)	1	1
Finely grated peeled gingerroot	1 tsp.	5 mL
Green onions, sliced	2	2

Marinade: Stir first 4 ingredients in small cup.

Make 4 or 5 deep diagonal slits in both sides of each fish. Place in shallow baking dish large enough to lay both fish flat. Pour marinade over fish, making sure to get some in slits. Turn to coat. Marinate at room temperature for 15 minutes. Drain well, discarding marinade. Blot dry with paper towels.

Coat fish in first amount of cornstarch.

Heat cooking oil in wok or large frying pan to 375°F (190°C). Carefully add 1 fish. Cook on medium-high for 2 minutes. Carefully turn fish away from you to avoid splashing yourself. Brown second side for about 2 minutes until fish flakes easily when tested with fork. Remove to paper towels to drain. Repeat with second fish.

Stir broth into second amount of cornstarch in separate small cup. Add chili sauce and water. Stir. Set aside.

(continued on next page)

Main Dishes

Heat sesame oil in small saucepan on medium. Add garlic and second amount of ginger. Stir for about 30 seconds until softened.

Add green onion. Stir for about 30 seconds until wilted. Stir cornstarch mixture. Stir into ginger mixture until boiling and thickened. Pour over fish. Serves 4.

1 serving: 247 Calories; 10 g Total Fat (4.7 g Mono, 2.7 g Poly, 1.7 g Sat); 65 mg Cholesterol; 12 g Carbohydrate; 1 g Fibre; 24 g Protein; 575 mg Sodium

Shrimp Ecstasy

A colourful, elegant dish with a delightful, mild curry flavour.

Water	1 tbsp.	15 mL
Cornstarch	2 tsp.	10 mL
Egg white (large)	1	1
Salt	3/4 tsp.	4 mL
Curry powder	1/2 tsp.	2 mL
Granulated sugar	1/2 tsp.	2 mL
Cooked medium shrimp	1 lb.	454 g
Cooking oil	1 tbsp.	15 mL
Medium onion, thinly sliced	1	1
Small red pepper, slivered	1	1
Green onions, cut into 2 inch (5 cm) pieces and slivered lengthwise	4	4

Stir water into cornstarch in medium bowl. Add next 4 ingredients. Stir.

Add shrimp. Stir. Let stand at room temperature for 30 minutes.

Heat wok or large frying pan on medium-high until very hot. Add cooking oil. Add sliced onion and red pepper. Stir-fry for 3 to 4 minutes until barely tender-crisp. Add shrimp mixture. Stir-fry for about 3 minutes until very hot.

Sprinkle with green onion. Makes 3 cups (750 mL). Serves 4.

1 serving: 176 Calories; 4.8 g Total Fat (2.3 g Mono, 1.6 g Poly, 0.6 g Sat); 221 mg Cholesterol; 7 g Carbohydrate; 1 g Fibre; 25 g Protein; 715 mg Sodium

Pictured on page 107.

Shrimp Omelet Stack

This unique-looking stack of omelets glistens with a wonderful thick, salty sauce. Yum! You may want to put the chopsticks aside for this dish.

Cooking oil	1 tbsp.	15 mL
Chopped fresh white mushrooms	1 cup	250 mL
Large eggs	8	8
Salt, just a pinch		
Pepper, just a pinch		
Raw medium shrimp, peeled and deveined, chopped	12 oz.	340 g
Fresh bean sprouts	1 cup	250 mL
Sliced green onion	1/2 cup	125 mL
Prepared chicken broth	1/4 cup	60 mL
Oyster sauce	2 tbsp.	30 mL
Soy sauce	1 tbsp.	15 mL
Water	1 tbsp.	15 mL
Cornstarch	2 tsp.	10 mL
Granulated sugar	1 tsp.	5 mL

Heat cooking oil in 8 inch (20 cm) frying pan on medium. Add mushrooms. Cook for about 3 minutes until mushrooms are browned. Transfer to small bowl.

Beat eggs, salt and pepper in medium bowl until frothy.

Add shrimp, bean sprouts, green onion and mushrooms. Mix well. Heat same greased frying pan on medium. Spoon 1/2 cup (125 mL) egg mixture into frying pan, swirling to coat bottom of pan. Cook for 1 to 2 minutes until bottom is browned. Turn omelet. Cook for about 1 minute until shrimp is pink. Remove to serving plate. Cover. Keep warm. Repeat with remaining egg mixture, stacking omelets on top of each other. Makes 6 omelets.

Combine remaining 6 ingredients in small saucepan. Heat and stir on medium until boiling and thickened. Pour over omelets. Cut into wedges. Serves 4 to 6.

1 serving: 288 Calories; 14.9 g Total Fat (6.1 g Mono, 2.9 g Poly, 3.7 g Sat); 528 mg Cholesterol; 10 g Carbohydrate; 1 g Fibre; 28 g Protein; 1280 mg Sodium

Pictured on page 144.

Garlic Shrimp And Broccoli

A tasty, healthy recipe that is so easy to prepare.
The thick, flavourful sauce coats the ingredients well.

Water	1 tbsp.	15 mL
Cornstarch	1 tbsp.	15 mL
Prepared chicken broth	1/4 cup	60 mL
Soy sauce	1 1/2 tbsp.	25 mL
Chinese barbecue sauce	1 1/2 tbsp.	25 mL
Sesame oil (optional)	1 tsp.	5 mL
Peanut (or cooking) oil	1 tbsp.	15 mL
Finely grated peeled gingerroot	1 tsp.	5 mL
Garlic cloves, minced (or 3/4 tsp., 4 mL, powder)	3	3
Sliced green onion	1/2 cup	125 mL
Broccoli florets	3 cups	750 mL
Raw medium shrimp, peeled and deveined	1 lb.	454 g

Stir water into cornstarch in small cup. Set aside.

Combine next 4 ingredients in small bowl.

Heat wok or large frying pan on medium-high until very hot. Add peanut oil. Add next 3 ingredients. Stir-fry for about 1 minute until fragrant.

Add broccoli and broth mixture. Stir-fry for about 2 minutes until broccoli is bright green.

Add shrimp. Stir-fry for about 3 minutes until shrimp are pink and broccoli is tender-crisp. Stir cornstarch mixture. Stir into shrimp mixture until boiling and thickened. Makes 3 1/2 cups (875 mL). Serves 4.

1 serving: 167 Calories; 5.4 g Total Fat (1.9 g Mono, 1.9 g Poly, 1 g Sat); 129 mg Cholesterol; 9 g Carbohydrate; 2 g Fibre; 21 g Protein; 639 mg Sodium

Pictured on page 108.

Paré Pointer
So much wok to be done!

Seafood In A Potato Nest

This is a special, beautifully presented dish that will be appreciated by those who love seafood. You may use any combination of seafood in this recipe as long as it adds up to a ready-to-use weight of 1 lb. (454 g).

Prepared chicken broth	1/2 cup	125 mL
Cornstarch	2 tsp.	10 mL
Dry sherry	2 tbsp.	30 mL
Water	1 tbsp.	15 mL
Raw lobster tails	9 oz.	255 g
Cooking oil	2 tbsp.	30 mL
Raw large shrimp, peeled and deveined, butterflied, blotted dry	5 oz.	140 g
Raw scallops, drained and cut in half if very large, blotted dry	4 oz.	113 g
Cooking oil	1 tbsp.	15 mL
Sliced water chestnuts, rinsed and drained	1/3 cup	75 mL
Black bean garlic sauce	2 tbsp.	30 mL
Finely grated peeled gingerroot	2 tsp.	10 mL
Green onions, sliced	3	3
Potato Nest (7 inch, 18 cm, size), page 119, warmed	1	1

Stir broth into cornstarch in small cup. Add sherry and water. Stir. Set aside.

Pull lobster meat from shell. Rinse. Cut into 1 inch (2.5 cm) pieces. Blot dry with paper towel.

Heat wok or large frying pan on medium-high until very hot. Add first amount of cooking oil. Add lobster, shrimp and scallops. Stir-fry for about 3 minutes until shrimp are pink and lobster and scallops are opaque. Do not overcook. Transfer to medium bowl. Keep warm.

(continued on next page)

Heat second amount of cooking oil in wok on medium. Add next 4 ingredients. Stir-fry for about 1 minute until fragrant. Stir cornstarch mixture. Stir into water chestnut mixture for about 1 minute until boiling and thickened. Add seafood and any juices. Heat and stir until heated through. Makes 3 1/3 cups (825 mL).

Spoon into warm potato nest. Serves 4.

1 serving: 368 Calories; 19.3 g Total Fat (10.8 g Mono, 5.7 g Poly, 1.5 g Sat); 95 mg Cholesterol; 25 g Carbohydrate; 2 g Fibre; 22 g Protein; 942 mg Sodium

Variation: Omit Potato Nest and spoon cooked seafood mixture into Mandarin Noodle Baskets, page 121.

Foo Yong Sauce

A smooth, brown sauce with a subtle green onion flavour.
The perfect complement to Chicken Foo Yong, page 73, Crab Foo Yong,
page 93, and Shrimp Foo Yong, page 102.

Water	1 cup	250 mL
Cornstarch	1 tbsp.	15 mL
Chicken bouillon powder	1 tbsp.	15 mL
Soy sauce	1 tsp.	5 mL
Granulated sugar	1/2 tsp.	2 mL
Green onions, finely sliced	2	2

Combine all 6 ingredients in small saucepan. Heat and stir on medium for about 4 minutes until boiling and thickened. Makes scant 1 cup (250 mL).

2 tbsp. (30 mL): 9 Calories; 0.2 g Total Fat (0.1 g Mono, 0.1 g Poly, trace Sat); trace Cholesterol; 2 g Carbohydrate; trace Fibre; trace Protein; 276 mg Sodium

---

Paré Pointer
Hi-ho, hi-ho, it's off to wok we go....

Shrimp Foo Yong

A nicely browned, pancake-like egg dish with visible
vegetables and a mild shrimp flavour.

Large eggs	8	8
Soy sauce	2 tsp.	10 mL
Salt	3/4 tsp.	4 mL
Pepper	1/4 tsp.	1 mL
Cooking oil	1 tbsp.	15 mL
Finely chopped fresh green beans	1 cup	250 mL
Chopped green pepper	1/4 cup	60 mL
Fresh bean sprouts, chopped once or twice	1 cup	250 mL
Cooked salad shrimp (about 5 oz., 140 g)	3/4 cup	175 mL
Sliced green onion	1/2 cup	125 mL
Cooking oil	1 1/2 tsp.	7 mL

Beat eggs, soy sauce, salt and pepper in medium bowl. Set aside.

Heat first amount of cooking oil in large frying pan on medium-high. Add green beans and green pepper. Stir-fry until softened.

Add bean sprouts, shrimp and green onion. Cook for 2 minutes. Cool slightly. Stir into egg mixture.

Heat 1/4 tsp. (1 mL) of second amount of cooking oil in frying pan on medium until hot. Spoon generous 1/3 cup (75 mL) egg mixture into frying pan. Cook for 1 to 2 minutes per side until lightly browned. Repeat for each omelet, using 1/4 tsp. (1 mL) cooking oil for each. Makes 6 omelets. Serves 4.

1 serving: 256 Calories; 15.7 g Total Fat (6.9 g Mono, 3.1 g Poly, 3.6 g Sat); 499 mg Cholesterol; 7 g Carbohydrate; 1 g Fibre; 22 g Protein; 829 mg Sodium

LOBSTER FOO YONG: When price is no object, omit shrimp and use same amount of lobster.

Paré Pointer
Just wok away.

Main Dishes

Honey Sesame Shrimp

The sweet, slightly nutty coating complements the fresh seafood flavour.
Tiny sesame seeds garnish these golden battered shrimp.

All-purpose flour	1 cup	250 mL
Cornstarch	1/4 cup	60 mL
Baking powder	2 tsp.	10 mL
Salt	1/2 tsp.	2 mL
Water	1 cup	250 mL
Large egg, fork-beaten	1	1
Soy sauce	2 tbsp.	30 mL
Raw large shrimp, peeled and deveined, blotted dry	1 1/2 lbs.	680 g
Cooking oil, for deep-frying		
Liquid honey	2 – 3 tbsp.	30 – 50 mL
Sesame seeds, toasted (see Tip, below)	1 tbsp.	15 mL

Measure first 4 ingredients into large bowl. Make a well in centre.

Add water, egg and soy sauce to well. Mix until smooth.

Put about 10 shrimp into batter. Mix until well coated. Remove with fork, letting excess batter drip back into bowl. Deep-fry in hot (375°F, 190°C) cooking oil for 2 to 3 minutes until golden. Remove with slotted spoon to paper towels to drain. Repeat with remaining shrimp and batter.

Heat large frying pan on medium-low. Add honey. Stir until warmed. Add shrimp. Toss until coated.

Sprinkle with sesame seeds. Serves 6.

1 serving: 621 Calories; 45.5 g Total Fat (25.6 g Mono, 13.6 g Poly, 3.7 g Sat); 180 mg Cholesterol;
30 g Carbohydrate; 1 g Fibre; 24 g Protein; 822 mg Sodium

 To toast nuts and seeds, place in single layer in ungreased shallow pan. Bake in 350°F (175°C) oven for 5 to 10 minutes, stirring or shaking often, until desired doneness.

Shrimp In Curry Sauce

Your guests will love this rich, fragrant dish.
The creamy sauce generously coats the tender shrimp.

Prepared chicken broth	1/4 cup	60 mL
Cornstarch	2 tsp.	10 mL
Dry sherry	2 tbsp.	30 mL
Soy sauce	2 tsp.	10 mL
Egg white (large)	1	1
Cornstarch	2 tsp.	10 mL
Salt	1/2 tsp.	2 mL
Raw medium shrimp, peeled and deveined, blotted dry	1 1/2 lbs.	680 g
Peanut (or cooking) oil	2 tbsp.	30 mL
Peanut (or cooking) oil (optional)	1 tbsp.	15 mL
Chopped onion	1/2 cup	125 mL
Garlic clove, minced (or 1/4 tsp., 1 mL, powder), optional	1	1
Curry powder	2 tsp.	10 mL
Whipping cream	1/4 cup	60 mL

Stir broth into first amount of cornstarch in small cup. Add sherry and soy sauce. Stir. Set aside.

Beat egg white, second amount of cornstarch and salt in medium bowl until frothy.

Add shrimp to egg white mixture. Stir until coated.

Heat wok or large frying pan on medium-high until very hot. Add first amount of peanut oil. Add shrimp. Stir-fry for about 1 minute until just pink. Do not overcook. Remove shrimp with slotted spoon to paper towels to drain, reserving any excess peanut oil in wok.

If peanut oil is absorbed and none remains in wok, add second amount of peanut oil. Heat wok on medium. Add onion, garlic and curry powder. Stir-fry for about 4 minutes until onion is soft and golden. Add shrimp. Stir cornstarch mixture. Stir into shrimp mixture for about 1 minute until boiling and slightly thickened.

(continued on next page)

Stir in whipping cream. Heat until boiling. Makes 2 1/2 cups (625 mL). Serves 6.

1 serving: 197 Calories; 9.8 g Total Fat (3.4 g Mono, 2.2 g Poly, 3.2 g Sat); 157 mg Cholesterol; 5 g Carbohydrate; trace Fibre; 21 g Protein; 503 mg Sodium

———

Steamed Fish

This moist, flaky fish has a hint of ginger and soy sauce. For a special occasion, serve on a decorative platter. I prefer head off in the kitchen.

Whole trout (or your choice) fish, pan ready	1 1/2 lbs.	680 g
Gingerroot slices (1/2 inch, 12 mm, thick), peeled and slivered into strips	2	2
Soy sauce	2 tsp.	10 mL
Sesame (or cooking) oil	2 tsp.	10 mL
Soy sauce	1 tsp.	5 mL
Chili sauce	1 tsp.	5 mL
Salt	1/4 tsp.	1 mL
Gingerroot slices (1/2 inch, 12 mm, thick), peeled and slivered into strips	3	3
Soy sauce	1 tbsp.	15 mL
Green onions, cut into 2 inch (5 cm) pieces and slivered lengthwise	4	4

Cut 3 crosswise slashes on each side of fish.

Mix first amounts of ginger and soy sauce on heatproof plate large enough to hold fish. Spread mixture over plate to match size of fish.

Combine next 4 ingredients in small cup. Rub into fish cavities. Set fish on plate.

Sprinkle with second amount of ginger. Drizzle with third amount of soy sauce. Place steamer rack in wok or steamer basket over boiling water that comes to within 1 inch (2.5 cm) of rack. Set plate with fish on rack. Cover. Steam for 15 to 20 minutes until fish flakes easily when thickest part is tested with fork.

Sprinkle with green onion. Serves 6 when served with other main course dishes.

1 serving: 189 Calories; 9.1 g Total Fat (4.3 g Mono, 2.3 g Poly, 1.5 g Sat); 66 mg Cholesterol; 1 g Carbohydrate; trace Fibre; 24 g Protein; 520 mg Sodium

Honey Five-Spice Ribs

These dark, glossy ribs are sticky and sweet. Perfectly cooked and seasoned with a wonderful array of ingredients, these are sure to become a favourite.

BARBECUE SAUCE

Chinese barbecue sauce	1/3 cup	75 mL
Water	1/4 cup	60 mL
Liquid honey	1/4 cup	60 mL
Dry sherry	1/4 cup	60 mL
Soy sauce	2 tbsp.	30 mL
Chili sauce	1 tbsp.	15 mL
Garlic cloves, minced (or 1 tsp., 5 mL, powder)	4	4
Chinese five-spice powder	1 tsp.	5 mL
Pork spareribs, cut into 2 – 3 rib portions	3 lbs.	1.4 kg
Pepper, generous sprinkle		
Water	1 cup	250 mL

Barbecue Sauce: Combine first 8 ingredients in small bowl. Makes 1 1/3 cups (325 mL) sauce.

Sprinkle ribs generously with pepper. Put into large roaster. Add second amount of water. Cover. Bake in 325°F (160°C) oven for about 1 1/2 hours until ribs are tender. Drain and discard liquid. Brush ribs with sauce. Return to roaster. Bake, uncovered, for about 1 hour, brushing with sauce several times, until ribs are glazed and tender. Serves 4 to 6.

1 serving: 739 Calories; 46.1 g Total Fat (19.9 g Mono, 4.3 g Poly, 17.3 g Sat); 175 mg Cholesterol; 28 g Carbohydrate; 2 g Fibre; 49 g Protein; 952 mg Sodium

Pictured on page 107.

1. Shrimp Ecstasy, page 97
2. Honey Five-Spice Ribs, above
3. Baby Bok Choy In Hoisin, page 133
4. Shrimp Crackers, page 25

Props Courtesy Of: X/S Wares

Sweet And Sour Pork

Tender pork, pineapple tidbits and green peppers combine in a tangy sweet and sour sauce. Serve the excess sauce over Steamed Rice, page 131.

White vinegar	3 tbsp.	50 mL
Cornstarch	4 tsp.	20 mL
Cooking oil	1 tbsp.	15 mL
Pork tenderloin, cut into 3/4 inch (2 cm) cubes	1 1/4 lbs.	560 g
Medium carrots, thinly sliced	2	2
Medium green pepper, cut into strips	1	1
Medium onion, coarsely chopped	1	1
Salt	1/2 tsp.	2 mL
Water	1/4 cup	60 mL
Can of pineapple tidbits (with juice)	14 oz.	398 mL
Brown sugar, packed	1/3 cup	75 mL
Soy sauce	1 1/2 tbsp.	25 mL

Stir vinegar into cornstarch in small cup. Set aside.

Heat wok or large frying pan on medium-high until very hot. Add cooking oil. Add pork. Stir-fry for about 5 minutes until lightly browned.

Add next 5 ingredients. Cover. Cook for about 3 minutes until vegetables are tender-crisp.

Add pineapple with juice, brown sugar and soy sauce. Stir. Stir cornstarch mixture. Stir into pork mixture for 3 to 4 minutes until boiling and thickened. Makes 6 cups (1.5 L). Serves 6.

1 serving: 283 Calories; 8.4 g Total Fat (4 g Mono, 1.4 g Poly, 2.2 g Sat); 60 mg Cholesterol; 32 g Carbohydrate; 2 g Fibre; 21 g Protein; 522 mg Sodium

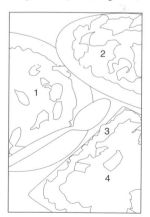

1. Suey Choy With Honey, page 136
2. Garlic Shrimp And Broccoli, page 99
3. Basic Pan-Fried Noodles, page 123
4. Cantonese Chow Mein, page 122

Props Courtesy Of: Danesco Inc.
Kitchen Treasures
X/S Wares

Main Dishes

Moo Shu Pork And Pancakes

The name "moo shu" is said to refer to the
bright yellow flower blossoms of the cassia (cinnamon) tree.
It may seem lengthy, but the results are well worth the extra effort.

MANDARIN PANCAKES

All-purpose flour	1 1/2 cups	375 mL
Salt	1 tsp.	5 mL
Sesame oil	1 tsp.	5 mL
Boiling water, approximately	1/2 cup	125 mL
Sesame oil	1 tbsp.	15 mL
Cooking oil	3 tbsp.	50 mL

FILLING

Dried black fungus (or 2 Chinese dried mushrooms)	1	1
Boilng water, to cover		
Prepared chicken broth	2 tbsp.	30 mL
Cornstarch	1 1/2 tsp.	7 mL
Soy sauce	1 tbsp.	15 mL
Dry sherry	1 1/2 tsp.	7 mL
Hoisin sauce	1 tsp.	5 mL
Large eggs	2	2
Granulated sugar	1/2 tsp.	2 mL
Salt	1/4 tsp.	1 mL
Cooking oil	1 1/2 tsp.	7 mL
Cooking oil	1 1/2 tsp.	7 mL
Boneless pork butt steak, trimmed of fat, thinly sliced and shredded	4 oz.	113 g
Garlic clove, minced (or 1/4 tsp., 1 mL, powder), optional	1	1
Finely grated peeled gingerroot (optional)	1/4 tsp.	1 mL
Fresh bean sprouts, chopped once or twice	2/3 cup	150 mL
Canned bamboo shoots, drained and cut julienne	1/4 cup	60 mL
Green onions, thinly sliced	2	2
Coarsely grated carrot	1 tbsp.	15 mL

(continued on next page)

Main Dishes

Mandarin Pancakes: Process flour, salt and first amount of sesame oil in food processor for 2 seconds.

With motor running, slowly pour boiling water through hole in lid until a ball starts to form. Gather dough together into ball. Knead on lightly floured surface until smooth, firm dough forms. Wrap loosely in plastic wrap. Let stand for 30 minutes. Form dough into 2 logs about 8 inches (20 cm) long. Cut each log into eight 1 inch (2.5 cm) portions. Keep dough covered with damp tea towel to prevent drying out. Roll portions into balls. Flatten dough balls, 1 at a time, between palms of hands.

Working with 2 pancakes at a time, brush surface of 1 with second amount of sesame oil. Place second pancake on top. Press down firmly. Roll both together with greased rolling pin out to 5 inch (12.5 cm) circle. Repeat with remaining dough, keeping pancakes covered with damp tea towel.

Heat large non-stick frying pan on medium-high until hot. Reduce heat to medium. Brush frying pan with cooking oil. Place 1 double pancake in frying pan. Cook for about 30 seconds per side until browned. Remove from pan and pull 2 pancakes apart while hot. Arrange on warm, lightly greased serving plate. Repeat with remaining pancakes. Keep warm.

Filling: Put fungus into small bowl. Add boiling water. Let stand for 20 minutes until softened. Remove and discard any tough pieces from fungus. Slice into about 2 inch (5 cm) long shreds. Set aside.

Stir broth into cornstarch in small cup. Add next 3 ingredients. Stir. Set aside.

Beat eggs, sugar and salt with fork in medium bowl. Heat large non-stick frying pan on medium-high until very hot. Add first amount of cooking oil. Add egg mixture. Scramble-fry until softly set. Return to bowl. Set aside. Wash frying pan if necessary.

Heat same frying pan on medium-high until very hot. Add second amount of cooking oil. Add pork, garlic, ginger and fungus. Stir-fry for 30 seconds.

Add remaining 4 ingredients. Stir-fry for 2 to 3 minutes until vegetables are tender-crisp. Stir cornstarch mixture. Stir into pork mixture for about 30 seconds until boiling and thickened. Add egg mixture. Scramble-fry until heated through. Makes about 1 1/2 cups (375 mL) filling. Fill pancakes with about 1 1/2 tbsp. (25 mL) filling. Fold in half or quarters to eat. Makes 16 filled pancakes.

1 filled pancake: 114 Calories; 6 g Total Fat (3 g Mono, 1.7 g Poly, 0.8 g Sat); 31 mg Cholesterol; 11 g Carbohydrate; 1 g Fibre; 4 g Protein; 279 mg Sodium

Pictured on page 90.

Frying Pan Pork Dumplings

These are traditionally served with a sprinkle of Chinese rice vinegar. Serve with
Sweet And Sour Sauce, page 15, or Hot Mustard Sauce, page 27.

Dried black fungus (or 4 Chinese dried mushrooms)	2	2
Boiling water, to cover		
Lean ground pork	12 oz.	340 g
Chopped canned bamboo shoots	1/4 cup	60 mL
Chopped green onion	1/4 cup	60 mL
Egg white (large)	1	1
Cornstarch	2 tbsp.	30 mL
Oyster sauce	1/4 cup	60 mL
Sesame oil	2 tsp.	10 mL
Finely grated peeled gingerroot	1 tsp.	5 mL
Chili paste (sambal oelek)	1/2 tsp.	2 mL
Pepper	1/4 tsp.	1 mL
Round dumpling wrappers	34	34
Cooking oil	2 tbsp.	30 mL
Hot water, approximately	2 2/3 cups	650 mL

Put fungus into small bowl. Add boiling water. Let stand for 20 minutes until softened. Drain. Remove and discard any tough pieces from fungus. Slice into about 2 inch (5 cm) long shreds.

Combine next 10 ingredients in large bowl. Mix well. Add fungus. Stir.

Place 1 tbsp. (15 mL) pork mixture in centre of dumpling wrapper. Dampen edges with water. Fold dumpling in half so edges almost come together. Fold edges together, pinch and pleat to form crescent shape. Tap bottom of dumpling on flat surface to stand upright. Repeat with remaining pork mixture and dumpling wrappers. Keep dumplings covered with damp tea towel to prevent drying out.

Measure 1 tbsp. (15 mL) cooking oil into large non-stick frying pan. Heat on medium until hot. Add 1/2 of dumplings to frying pan in single layer. Cook for about 2 minutes until bottom is browned. Slowly add 1 1/3 cups (325 mL) hot water to frying pan. Cover. Cook for about 15 minutes until water is evaporated and dumplings are soft and cooked. If water evaporates before 15 minutes cooking time, add a little more to keep dumplings steaming. Repeat with remaining dumplings, cooking oil and hot water. Makes 34 dumplings.

(continued on next page)

Main Dishes

1 dumpling: 53 Calories; 1.8 g Total Fat (0.9 g Mono, 0.5 g Poly, 0.3 g Sat); 7 mg Cholesterol; 6 g Carbohydrate; trace Fibre; 3 g Protein; 228 mg Sodium

---

Lychee Pork

Lychee lovers will delight in the flavour of this sweet dish. Its unique appearance will add interest to your dinner table and it goes very well with rice.

All-purpose flour	1 1/3 cups	325 mL
Salt	2 tsp.	10 mL
Large eggs	3	3
Pork tenderloin, cut into 3/4 inch (2 cm) cubes	1 1/2 lbs.	680 g
Cooking oil, for deep-frying		
Can of lychee fruit (with syrup)	20 oz.	565 mL
White vinegar	1/4 cup	60 mL
Granulated sugar	2 tbsp.	30 mL
Dry sherry	2 tbsp.	30 mL
Ketchup	2 tbsp.	30 mL
Soy sauce	1 tbsp.	15 mL
Water	2 tbsp.	30 mL
Cornstarch	1 1/2 tbsp.	25 mL

Stir flour and salt in medium bowl.

Beat eggs with fork in small bowl.

Dip pork, a few pieces at a time, into egg. Roll in flour mixture until coated.

Deep-fry, in 3 batches, in hot (375°F, 190°C) cooking oil for about 6 minutes, stirring several times to separate pieces, until browned and cooked through. Remove to paper towels to drain. Transfer to serving dish. Keep warm.

Combine next 6 ingredients in medium saucepan. Bring to a boil.

Stir water into cornstarch in small cup. Stir into lychee mixture until thickened. Pour over pork. Stir lightly until combined. Serves 6.

1 serving: 554 Calories; 28.7 g Total Fat (15.1 g Mono, 6.7 g Poly, 4.3 g Sat); 175 mg Cholesterol; 44 g Carbohydrate; 1 g Fibre; 30 g Protein; 1100 mg Sodium

Sweet And Sour Ribs

This bright, colourful dish is delicious!

SWEET AND SOUR SAUCE

Reserved pineapple juice	1/4 cup	60 mL
Cornstarch	2 tsp.	10 mL
Ketchup	1/3 cup	75 mL
White vinegar	3 tbsp.	50 mL
Dry sherry	2 tbsp.	30 mL
Water	1 tbsp.	15 mL
Granulated sugar	2 tbsp.	30 mL
Soy sauce	2 tbsp.	30 mL
Egg yolk (large)	1	1
Sweet and sour cut pork ribs, cut into 1-bone portions	3 lbs.	1.4 kg
Cornstarch	1/2 cup	125 mL
Cooking oil, for deep-frying		
Cooking oil	1 tbsp.	15 mL
Medium onion, cut into thin wedges	1	1
Can of pineapple tidbits, drained and 1/4 cup (60 mL) juice reserved	14 oz.	398 mL
Chopped red pepper	1 cup	250 mL

Sweet And Sour Sauce: Stir pineapple juice into first amount of cornstarch in small bowl. Add next 4 ingredients. Stir. Set aside.

Combine sugar, soy sauce and egg yolk in medium bowl. Add pork. Toss until coated. Marinate in refrigerator for 1 hour.

Coat each piece of drained pork with second amount of cornstarch. Deep-fry in hot (350°F, 175°C) cooking oil for about 3 minutes until golden brown and pork is cooked. Remove to paper towels to drain.

Heat wok or large frying pan on medium-high until very hot. Add second amount of cooking oil. Add onion. Stir-fry for about 3 minutes until onion is softened.

Add pineapple, red pepper and pork. Stir sauce. Add to pork mixture. Stir-fry until pork is coated and heated through. Makes 8 cups (2 L).

1 cup (250 mL): 521 Calories; 34.9 g Total Fat (16.8 g Mono, 5.6 g Poly, 9.7 g Sat); 115 mg Cholesterol; 26 g Carbohydrate; 1 g Fibre; 25 g Protein; 484 mg Sodium

Pictured on page 126.

Mongolian Lamb

These tender strips of lamb are coated in a savoury sauce.
Serve with Steamed Rice, page 131.

Large egg	1	1
Low-sodium soy sauce	2 tbsp.	30 mL
Black bean sauce	1 tbsp.	15 mL
Cornstarch	2 tsp.	10 mL
Chinese chili sauce	1 tsp.	5 mL
Chinese five-spice powder	1/4 – 1/2 tsp.	1 – 2 mL
Garlic clove, minced (or 1/4 tsp., 1 mL, powder)	1	1
Lean boneless lamb, thinly sliced	1 1/2 lbs.	680 g
Prepared chicken broth	1/4 cup	60 mL
Cornstarch	2 tsp.	10 mL
Low-sodium soy sauce	1 tbsp.	15 mL
Water	1 tbsp.	15 mL
Sesame oil	1/2 tsp.	2 mL
Cooking oil	1 tbsp.	15 mL
Medium onions, sliced into 8 wedges each	2	2
Cooking oil	1 tbsp.	15 mL
Green onion, thinly sliced	1	1

Beat egg with fork in large bowl. Add next 6 ingredients. Stir. Add lamb. Stir. Cover. Marinate in refrigerator for 1 hour.

Stir broth into second amount of cornstarch in small bowl. Add next 3 ingredients. Stir. Set aside.

Heat wok or large frying pan on medium-high until very hot. Add first amount of cooking oil. Add onion wedges. Stir-fry for about 5 minutes until just softened and beginning to brown. Transfer to separate small bowl. Cover. Keep warm.

Heat second amount of cooking oil in wok. Stir-fry lamb and marinade, in 2 batches, for 2 to 3 minutes until lamb is browned. Add onion wedges. Stir broth mixture. Stir into lamb mixture for about 3 minutes until boiling and thickened.

Sprinkle with green onion. Makes 4 cups (1 L).

1 cup (250 mL): 377 Calories; 19.4 g Total Fat (9.1 g Mono, 3.5 g Poly, 4.7 g Sat); 166 mg Cholesterol; 10 g Carbohydrate; 1 g Fibre; 39 g Protein; 709 mg Sodium

Diced Tofu And Noodles

Red and green peppers add colour and texture to this mildly flavoured noodle dish. Use more chili paste if you like it hot. For a twist, try using Basic Pan-Fried Noodles, page 123, in place of the boiled noodles in this recipe.

Package of extra-firm tofu	12 1/4 oz.	350 g
Apple juice	3/4 cup	175 mL
Garlic clove, minced (or 1/4 tsp., 1 mL, powder)	1	1
Apple cider vinegar	1 tbsp.	15 mL
Soy sauce	1 tbsp.	15 mL
Chili paste (sambal oelek)	1/2 tsp.	2 mL
Cornstarch	1 tbsp.	15 mL
Package of instant Chinese noodles (14 oz., 400 g, size)	1/2	1/2
Boiling water	12 cups	3 L
Salt	2 tsp.	10 mL
Sesame oil	1 tsp.	5 mL
Cooking oil	2 tbsp.	30 mL
Can of baby corn, drained and cut into 1 1/2 inch (3.8 cm) pieces	14 oz.	398 mL
Sliced fresh white mushrooms	1 cup	250 mL
Chopped onion	1 cup	250 mL
Diced green pepper	1/2 cup	125 mL
Diced red pepper	1/2 cup	125 mL
Salt, sprinkle		
Pepper, sprinkle		

Cover baking sheet with double thickness of paper towel. Place tofu on top. Cover with double thickness of paper towel. Tilt pan slightly. Place another pan on top. Place canned goods or heavy pot on top to press tofu. Let stand for at least 20 minutes to drain. Cut tofu into 1/2 inch (12 mm) cubes.

Combine next 5 ingredients in medium bowl. Add tofu. Stir until coated. Marinate at room temperature for 1 hour, stirring gently once or twice. Drain tofu through sieve, reserving apple juice mixture in small bowl. Set tofu aside.

(continued on next page)

Main Dishes

Stir apple juice mixture into cornstarch in separate small bowl. Set aside.

Cook noodles in boiling water and salt in large uncovered pot or Dutch oven for 4 to 6 minutes until tender but firm. Drain. Return to pot. Add sesame oil. Toss to coat. Keep warm.

Heat wok or large frying pan on medium-high until very hot. Add cooking oil. Add remaining 7 ingredients. Stir-fry for about 2 minutes until tender-crisp. Stir apple juice mixture. Stir into vegetable mixture until boiling and thickened. Add tofu. Stir gently until heated through. Arrange noodles on platter. Top with tofu mixture. Makes 8 cups (2 L). Serves 4.

1 serving: 497 Calories; 18.3 g Total Fat (6.9 g Mono, 7.6 g Poly, 2.3 g Sat); 48 mg Cholesterol; 65 g Carbohydrate; 5 g Fibre; 24 g Protein; 416 mg Sodium

Pictured on page 89.

Fried Crumbed Tofu

These crunchy, golden tofu rectangles have a mild garlic flavour with a hint of curry and cayenne pepper. Use the higher amount of cayenne for more of a kick.

Fine dry bread crumbs	1/4 cup	60 mL
Salt	1/4 tsp.	1 mL
Curry powder	1/8 tsp.	0.5 mL
Garlic powder	1/8 tsp.	0.5 mL
Cayenne pepper	1/8 – 1/4 tsp.	0.5 – 1 mL
Medium or firm tofu	1 lb.	454 g
Cooking oil	1 tbsp.	15 mL

Combine first 5 ingredients in small bowl.

Cut tofu into 1/2 inch (1.2 cm) thick slices, then into 3 x 1 inch (7.5 x 2.5 cm) pieces. Gently press each piece into crumb mixture until coated.

Cook tofu, in 2 batches, in cooking oil in frying pan on medium, turning to brown both sides. Makes 27 pieces.

1 piece: 33 Calories; 2 g Total Fat (0.7 g Mono, 1 g Poly, 0.3 g Sat); 0 mg Cholesterol; 2 g Carbohydrate; trace Fibre; 3 g Protein; 34 mg Sodium

Beef Satay Noodles

You'll enjoy the mild peanut butter
flavour of this dish and its hot, citrusy aftertaste.

Medium rice stick noodles	8 oz.	225 g
Boiling water	12 cups	3 L
Garlic cloves, minced (or 1/2 tsp., 2 mL, powder)	2	2
Soy sauce	1 tbsp.	15 mL
Brown sugar, packed	1 tsp.	5 mL
Chili paste (sambal oelek)	1/2 tsp.	2 mL
Beef tenderloin steak, cut julienne	7 oz.	200 g
Prepared beef broth	1/2 cup	125 mL
Cornstarch	1 tsp.	5 mL
Dry sherry	1 tbsp.	15 mL
Soy sauce	1 tbsp.	15 mL
Lemon juice	1 tsp.	5 mL
Salt	1/2 tsp.	2 mL
Dried crushed chilies	1/4 tsp.	1 mL
Cooking oil	2 tbsp.	30 mL
Peanut butter	2 tbsp.	30 mL
Chopped green onion	1/4 cup	60 mL
Finely chopped roasted peanuts	1 tbsp.	15 mL

Cook noodles in boiling water in large uncovered pot or Dutch oven for about 5 minutes until tender but firm. Drain. Rinse with cold water. Drain. Set aside.

Combine next 4 ingredients in small bowl. Add beef. Stir until coated. Marinate at room temperature for 10 minutes.

Stir broth into cornstarch in small cup. Add next 5 ingredients. Stir. Set aside.

Heat wok or large frying pan on medium-high until very hot. Add cooking oil. Add beef and marinade. Stir-fry for 1 minute.

Add peanut butter and green onion. Stir-fry for about 30 seconds until peanut butter is melted. Stir cornstarch mixture. Stir into beef mixture for about 3 minutes until boiling and slightly thickened. Add noodles. Heat and stir until noodles are lightly coated with sauce and heated through.

(continued on next page)

118

Sprinkle with peanuts just before serving. Makes 5 cups (1.25 L). Serves 4.

1 serving: 448 Calories; 16.4 g Total Fat (8 g Mono, 3.7 g Poly, 2.9 g Sat); 25 mg Cholesterol; 56 g Carbohydrate; 2 g Fibre; 19 g Protein; 996 mg Sodium

Potato Nest

This crisp, golden potato bowl has a tasty potato chip flavour. This is an attractive way to serve colourful Chinese dishes. Break off chunks of the nest to eat.

Cornstarch	1/4 cup	60 mL
Salt	1/2 tsp.	2 mL
Medium baking potatoes, peeled and cut julienne (or coarsely grated into 2 – 3 inch, 5 – 7.5 cm, shreds), about 2 1/3 cups (575 mL)	2	2
Cooking oil, for deep-frying	8 cups	2 L

Combine cornstarch and salt in large bowl.

Add potato. Toss until coated. Place in 8 inch (20 cm) wire mesh basket with long handles. Press another 8 inch (20 cm) wire mesh basket on top, forcing potato into bowl shape.

Heat cooking oil in wok or large wide pot to 375°F (190°C). Holding both handles together, slowly submerge baskets into cooking oil. Hold and cook for 2 minutes. Release handle and cook for 8 to 10 minutes until golden brown. Remove to paper towels to drain. While still warm, carefully loosen potato from basket with knife. Serves 4.

1 serving: 333 Calories; 29.1 g Total Fat (17.1 g Mono, 8.6 g Poly, 2.1 g Sat); 0 mg Cholesterol; 18 g Carbohydrate; 1 g Fibre; 1 g Protein; 301 mg Sodium

Pictured on page 125.

SMALL POTATO NESTS: You can make 2 smaller nests for individual presentations by cooking 1/2 amount of potato using 5 1/2 inch (14 cm) skimmer baskets. Cook for 1 minute. Remove top skimmer basket. Cook for about 5 minutes until golden brown.

Chicken Chow Mein

You've probably tasted this classic before in your favourite Chinese restaurant!

Package of instant Chinese noodles (14 oz., 400 g, size)	1/2	1/2
Boiling water	12 cups	3 L
Salt	1 tbsp.	15 mL
Chinese dried mushrooms	3	3
Boiling water	1/2 cup	125 mL
Prepared chicken broth	1/2 cup	125 mL
Cornstarch	2 tsp.	10 mL
Soy sauce	2 tbsp.	30 mL
Oyster sauce	2 tbsp.	30 mL
Dry sherry	2 tbsp.	30 mL
Cooking oil	1 tbsp.	15 mL
Boneless, skinless chicken breast halves (4 oz., 113 g, each), cut into thin 2 inch (5 cm) long strips	2	2
Garlic clove, minced (or 1/4 tsp., 1 mL, powder)	1	1
Cooking oil	1 tbsp.	15 mL
Coarsely shredded suey choy (Chinese cabbage), lightly packed	1 cup	250 mL
Medium onion, cut into wedges	1	1
Diced celery	1/2 cup	125 mL
Chow mein noodles (optional)	1/2 cup	125 mL

Cook Chinese noodles in boiling water and salt in large uncovered pot or Dutch oven for about 5 minutes until tender but firm. Drain. Rinse with cold water. Drain well.

Put mushrooms into small bowl. Add boiling water. Let stand for 20 minutes until softened. Remove mushrooms, reserving liquid. Strain liquid through fine cloth or several layers of cheesecloth. Reserve. Remove and discard stems. Slice caps thinly. Set aside.

Combine next 5 ingredients and reserved mushroom liquid in separate small bowl. Set aside.

(continued on next page)

Heat wok or large frying pan on medium-high until very hot. Add first amount of cooking oil. Add chicken, garlic and mushrooms. Stir-fry for about 3 minutes until chicken is no longer pink. Transfer to medium bowl.

Heat second amount of cooking oil in wok. Add suey choy, onion and celery. Stir-fry for about 2 minutes until tender-crisp. Add chicken mixture. Stir cornstarch mixture. Stir into chicken mixture for about 1 minute until boiling and thickened. Add Chinese noodles. Heat and stir for 3 to 4 minutes until heated through.

Sprinkle with chow mein noodles just before serving. Makes 5 1/2 cups (1.4 L). Serves 4.

1 serving: 370 Calories; 10.4 g Total Fat (5.1 g Mono, 2.9 g Poly, 1.3 g Sat); 80 mg Cholesterol; 46 g Carbohydrate; 3 g Fibre; 22 g Protein; 1394 mg Sodium

---

Mandarin Noodle Baskets

This is a fun, creative way to serve stir-fries. Break off chunks of the basket to eat. The baskets can be made a day ahead and stored in an airtight container in a cool, dry place. You can purchase the wire baskets from an Asian grocery or kitchen supply store.

Package of fresh thick yellow noodles (Mandarin noodles)	**1 lb.**	**454 g**

Cooking oil, for deep-frying

Separate noodles. Place 1/2 of noodles in 8 inch (20 cm) wire mesh basket with long handles. Press another 8 inch (20 cm) wire mesh basket on top, forcing noodles into bowl shape.

Heat cooking oil in wok or large wide pot to 375°F (190°C). Holding both handles together, submerge baskets into cooking oil. Hold and cook for 2 to 3 minutes until crisp and golden. Remove to paper towels to drain. While still warm, carefully loosen noodles from basket with knife. Repeat with remaining noodles. Serves 8.

1 serving: 198 Calories; 14.7 g Total Fat (8.4 g Mono, 4.3 g Poly, 1.2 g Sat); 19 mg Cholesterol; 14 g Carbohydrate; 1 g Fibre; 3 g Protein; 94 mg Sodium

Pictured on page 125.

Cantonese Chow Mein

Colourful, well-seasoned vegetables top these delicious thin noodles. This is a bright, fresh-looking dish that will liven up your dinner table.

Prepared chicken broth	1 cup	250 mL
Cornstarch	4 tsp.	20 mL
Dry sherry	3 tbsp.	50 mL
Soy sauce	2 tbsp.	30 mL
Chili black bean sauce	1 tsp.	5 mL
Cooking oil	1 tbsp.	15 mL
Lean ground pork	5 oz.	140 g
Garlic cloves, minced (or 3/4 tsp., 4 mL, powder)	3	3
Cubed red pepper	1 cup	250 mL
Small fresh button mushrooms	1 cup	250 mL
Diced celery	3/4 cup	175 mL
Fresh pea pods	1 cup	250 mL
Green onions, thinly sliced	5	5
Basic Pan-Fried Noodles, page 123, warmed	1	1
Green onions, sliced, for garnish	2	2

Stir broth into cornstarch in small cup. Add next 3 ingredients. Stir. Set aside.

Heat wok or large frying pan on medium-high until very hot. Add cooking oil. Add ground pork and garlic. Stir-fry for 1 minute.

Add red pepper, mushrooms and celery. Stir-fry for 2 minutes.

Add pea pods and first amount of green onion. Stir-fry for 1 minute. Stir cornstarch mixture. Stir into vegetable mixture until boiling and thickened.

Arrange noodles on serving plate. Cover with vegetable mixture. Garnish with second amount of green onion. Serves 4.

1 serving: 281 Calories; 12.3 g Total Fat (6.5 g Mono, 3.3 g Poly, 1.7 g Sat); 40 mg Cholesterol; 27 g Carbohydrate; 3 g Fibre; 15 g Protein; 1268 mg Sodium

Pictured on page 108.

Basic Pan-Fried Noodles

These simple, golden noodles are flavoured with soy sauce. Use them as a bed for stir-fried and cooked dishes or enjoy them on their own.

Fresh Chinese egg noodles	8 oz.	225 g
Boiling water	10 cups	2.5 L
Cooking oil	1 1/2 tbsp.	25 mL
Soy sauce	2 tsp.	10 mL
Salt	1/4 tsp.	1 mL

Cook noodles in boiling water in large uncovered pot or Dutch oven for about 2 minutes until tender but firm. Remove from heat. Stir to loosen noodles. Drain well.

Heat large non-stick frying pan on medium until very hot. Add cooking oil. Add noodles and soy sauce. Mix well. Flatten into even layer on bottom of frying pan. Cook for 3 to 5 minutes, adjusting heat as necessary to prevent burning, until golden brown on bottom. Slide noodles out of frying pan onto plate. Cover with another plate. Invert. Slide noodles back into frying pan on unbrowned side.

Sprinkle with salt. Cook for 3 to 4 minutes until noodles are crisp and golden. Serves 4.

1 serving: 123 Calories; 6 g Total Fat (3.3 g Mono, 1.8 g Poly, 0.5 g Sat); 19 mg Cholesterol; 14 g Carbohydrate; 1 g Fibre; 3 g Protein; 415 mg Sodium

Pictured on page 108.

Paré Pointer

Wok up and smell the coffee.

Shanghai Noodles

These noodles are quick and so easy to prepare!
This spicy dish would go very well with a chicken stir-fry.

Fresh Chinese egg noodles	12 oz.	340 g
Boiling water	12 cups	3 L
Peanut (or cooking) oil	1 tbsp.	15 mL
Medium onion, cut into thin wedges	1	1
Chopped red pepper	1 cup	250 mL
Chopped green onion	1/2 cup	125 mL
Chinese satay sauce	1/4 cup	60 mL
Prepared chicken broth	1/4 cup	60 mL
Soy sauce	2 tbsp.	30 mL
Sesame oil (optional)	2 tsp.	10 mL

Cook noodles in boiling water in large uncovered pot or Dutch oven for about 2 minutes until tender but firm. Remove from heat. Stir to loosen noodles. Drain. Rinse with cold water. Drain well. Set aside.

Heat wok or large frying pan on medium-high until very hot. Add peanut oil. Add next 4 ingredients. Stir-fry for about 1 minute until fragrant.

Add noodles and remaining 3 ingredients. Stir-fry for 3 to 5 minutes until hot and onion is tender-crisp. Makes about 6 1/2 cups (1.6 L).

1 cup (250 mL): 145 Calories; 6.1 g Total Fat (2.5 g Mono, 1.7 g Poly, 1.5 g Sat); 17 mg Cholesterol; 18 g Carbohydrate; 2 g Fibre; 5 g Protein; 626 mg Sodium

1. Bird's Nest Chicken, page 84
2. Potato Nest, page 119
3. Orange Beef And Broccoli, page 58
4. Mandarin Noodle Baskets, page 121

Props Courtesy Of: Chintz & Company
Pier 1 Imports

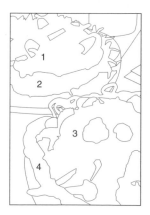

Mushroom Fried Rice

Mushroom fans will love this easy, satisfying rice dish.

Cooking oil	1 1/2 tbsp.	25 mL
Cold cooked long grain white rice	3 cups	750 mL
(about 1 cup, 250 mL, uncooked)		
Large eggs, beaten until frothy	2	2
Sliced fresh white mushrooms	2 cups	500 mL
Sliced green onion	1/2 cup	125 mL
Cooked deli ham slices, cut into 2 inch	2	2
(5 cm) slivers		
Soy sauce	1 1/2 tbsp.	25 mL
Pepper	1/8 tsp.	0.5 mL

Heat cooking oil in large non-stick frying pan on medium. Add rice. Heat, stirring occasionally, for 5 to 10 minutes until broken up into individual grains and hot.

Add egg. Stir until set.

Add next 3 ingredients. Stir-fry for 3 to 5 minutes until mushrooms are softened.

Add soy sauce and pepper. Stir-fry until well mixed. Makes 3 cups (750 mL).

1/2 cup (125 mL): 227 Calories; 6.5 g Total Fat (3.2 g Mono, 1.5 g Poly, 1.2 g Sat); 78 mg Cholesterol; 33 g Carbohydrate; 1 g Fibre; 8 g Protein; 437 mg Sodium

Pictured on page 54.

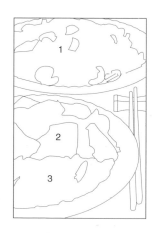

1. Braised Vegetables, page 135
2. Sweet And Sour Ribs, page 114
3. Ham Fried Rice, page 129

Props Courtesy Of: Chintz & Company
Pier 1 Imports

Yangtze Fried Rice

A delicious fried rice recipe that will go well with any meal.
The fresh, colourful vegetables add colour and texture to the dish.

Chinese dried mushrooms	4	4
Boiling water, to cover		
Cooking oil	2 tbsp.	30 mL
Large eggs	3	3
Cold cooked long grain white rice	3 cups	750 mL
(about 1 cup, 250 mL, uncooked)		
Soy sauce	2 tbsp.	30 mL
Finely diced cooked ham	1/2 cup	125 mL
Frozen peas, thawed and drained	1/2 cup	125 mL
Cooked salad shrimp	1/2 cup	125 mL
Diced cooked carrot	1/2 cup	125 mL
Green onions, finely chopped	2	2

Put mushrooms into small bowl. Add boiling water. Let stand for 20 minutes until softened. Drain. Remove and discard stems. Slice caps finely. Set aside.

Heat wok or large frying pan on medium until hot. Add cooking oil. Add eggs. Break yolks. Cook, without stirring, for 2 minutes. Flip. Immediately start chopping egg with edge of pancake lifter until egg is in small pieces and starting to brown.

Add rice and soy sauce. Stir-fry, breaking up rice, for about 5 minutes until dry and starting to brown.

Add mushrooms and remaining 5 ingredients. Stir-fry for about 5 minutes until heated through. Makes 5 cups (1.25 L). Serves 6.

1 serving: 279 Calories; 8.7 g Total Fat (4.3 g Mono, 2 g Poly, 1.6 g Sat); 139 mg Cholesterol; 37 g Carbohydrate; 2 g Fibre; 13 g Protein; 591 mg Sodium

Pictured on page 18 and on back cover.

Ham Fried Rice

Tender strands of carrot and smoky slivers of ham
add colour and flavour to this rice dish.

Cooking oil	3 tbsp.	50 mL
Finely chopped onion	1 cup	250 mL
Grated carrot	1/2 cup	125 mL
Large eggs, beaten until frothy	3	3
Cold cooked long grain white rice (about 1 1/3 cups, 325 mL, uncooked)	4 cups	1 L
Slivered cooked ham	3/4 cup	175 mL
Green onions, chopped	2	2
Soy sauce	3 tbsp.	50 mL
Dry sherry	1 tsp.	5 mL

Heat wok or large frying pan on medium-high until very hot. Add cooking oil. Add onion and carrot. Stir-fry for about 2 minutes until onion is softened.

Add egg. Stir-fry for about 30 seconds until partially set.

Add rice, quickly breaking up. Stir well until rice is coated.

Add ham and green onion. Stir-fry for 2 to 3 minutes until well mixed and heated through.

Add soy sauce and sherry. Stir-fry for about 1 minute until well mixed. Makes 5 cups (1.25 L). Serves 6.

1 serving: 338 Calories; 11.4 g Total Fat (5.9 g Mono, 2.7 g Poly, 1.9 g Sat); 118 mg Cholesterol; 46 g Carbohydrate; 1 g Fibre; 12 g Protein; 797 mg Sodium

Pictured on page 126.

Paré Pointer
Caught between a wok and a hard place?

Egg Foo Yong

*Crunchy bean sprouts and green onion flecks add interest to
these brown egg cakes. Drizzle with Foo Yong Sauce,
page 101, for a wonderful, exotic flavour.*

Cooking oil	1 tbsp.	15 mL
Medium green pepper, chopped	1	1
Green onions, sliced	5	5
Chopped fresh white mushrooms	1/2 cup	125 mL
Fresh bean sprouts, chopped once or twice	1 1/2 cups	375 mL
Canned bamboo shoots, drained, rinsed and slivered	1/4 cup	60 mL
Cold cooked long grain white rice (about 3/4 cup, 175 mL, uncooked)	1 1/2 cups	375 mL
Large eggs	4	4
Soy sauce	2 tbsp.	30 mL
Dry sherry	1 tbsp.	15 mL
Sesame oil (optional)	1 tsp.	5 mL
Salt	3/4 tsp.	4 mL
White (or black) pepper	1/8 tsp.	0.5 mL
Cooking oil	1 tbsp.	15 mL

Heat first amount of cooking oil in large non-stick frying pan on medium until hot. Add green pepper, green onion and mushrooms. Cook for about 2 minutes until green pepper is softened and liquid from mushrooms is evaporated.

Add bean sprouts and bamboo shoots. Stir-fry for about 1 minute until bean sprouts are tender-crisp. Transfer to large bowl. Add rice. Stir.

Beat next 6 ingredients in small bowl. Add to rice mixture. Stir.

Heat 1 tsp. (5 mL) of second amount of cooking oil in same frying pan on medium-low. Spoon 1/4 cup (60 mL) rice mixture into frying pan for each cake. Cook for about 3 minutes until almost set and bottom is lightly browned. Turn. Cook for about 2 minutes until browned. Repeat with remaining cooking oil and rice mixture. Makes 12 cakes.

*1 cake: 88 Calories; 4.1 g Total Fat (2 g Mono, 1 g Poly, 0.7 g Sat); 72 mg Cholesterol;
9 g Carbohydrate; 1 g Fibre; 4 g Protein; 346 mg Sodium*

Steamed Rice

Fluffy white rice with a natural flavour and an appetizing texture.
A great accompaniment to any stir-fry or cooked dish.

Water	2 1/4 cups	550 mL
Long grain white rice	1 1/2 cups	375 mL

Put water and rice into medium saucepan. Stir. Bring to a boil. Reduce heat to low. Cover. Cook for 15 minutes. Remove from heat. Let stand for 5 minutes. Fluff with fork. Makes about 5 cups (1.25 L).

1/2 cup (125 mL): 107 Calories; 0.2 g Total Fat (0.1 g Mono, 0.1 g Poly, 0.1 g Sat); 0 mg Cholesterol; 23 g Carbohydrate; trace Fibre; 2 g Protein; 1 mg Sodium

Pictured on page 71.

 For fried rice, we use the term "cold" when referring to cooked long grain rice. Using leftover cold (room temperature) rice is important in fried rice because of the texture. Hot rice will still absorb some of the liquid in the dish, becoming soft and mushy. If you are using leftover cold cooked rice, wet hands to prevent rice sticking to you and squeeze rice gently to break apart.

Chinese Pea Pods

*Bright green pea pods and crunchy water chestnuts
are coated in a mild, slightly sweet sauce.*

Water	1/2 cup	125 mL
Cornstarch	1 tbsp.	15 mL
Dry sherry	2 tbsp.	30 mL
Soy sauce	1 tbsp.	15 mL
Chicken bouillon powder	1 1/2 tsp.	7 mL
Granulated sugar	1 tsp.	5 mL
Salt	1/2 tsp.	2 mL
Cooking oil	2 tbsp.	30 mL
Medium onion, halved lengthwise and sliced	1	1
Can of sliced water chestnuts, drained	8 oz.	227 mL
Fresh pea pods	2 1/4 cups	550 mL

Stir water into cornstarch in small bowl. Add next 5 ingredients. Stir. Set aside.

Heat wok or large frying pan on medium-high until very hot. Add cooking oil. Add onion and water chestnuts. Stir-fry for about 1 minute until starting to soften.

Add pea pods. Stir-fry for 1 to 2 minutes until bright green. Stir cornstarch mixture. Stir into pea pod mixture until boiling and thickened. Makes 3 1/2 cups (875 mL). Serves 4.

1 serving: 174 Calories; 7.4 g Total Fat (4.2 g Mono, 2.2 g Poly, 0.6 g Sat); trace Cholesterol; 22 g Carbohydrate; 3 g Fibre; 5 g Protein; 811 mg Sodium

Paré Pointer
With a wiggle in her wok and a giggle in her talk....

Vegetable Dishes

Baby Bok Choy In Hoisin

An attractive dish with a savoury sauce
that enhances the fresh flavour of the bok choy.

Prepared chicken broth	1/3 cup	75 mL
Cornstarch	1 tsp.	5 mL
Hoisin sauce	2 tbsp.	30 mL
Ketchup	2 tsp.	10 mL
Dried crushed chilies	1/4 tsp.	1 mL
Cooking oil	1 tbsp.	15 mL
Sliced fresh white mushrooms	1 cup	250 mL
Garlic cloves, minced (or 1/2 tsp., 2 mL, powder)	2	2
Heads of baby bok choy (about 1 1/2 lbs., 680 g), chopped	8	8
Green onions, cut into 2 inch (5 cm) pieces	3	3
Sesame seeds, toasted (see Tip, page 103)	1 tsp.	5 mL

Stir broth into cornstarch in small bowl. Add next 3 ingredients. Stir. Set aside.

Heat wok or large frying pan on medium-high until very hot. Add cooking oil. Add mushrooms and garlic. Stir-fry for 30 seconds. Add bok choy and green onion. Stir-fry for 2 to 3 minutes until tender-crisp. Stir broth mixture. Stir into bok choy mixture for about 1 minute until boiling and thickened. Do not overcook.

Sprinkle with sesame seeds just before serving. Makes about 7 1/2 cups (1.9 L). Serves 6.

1 serving: 64 Calories; 3 g Total Fat (1.5 g Mono, 1 g Poly, 0.3 g Sat); 0 mg Cholesterol; 8 g Carbohydrate; 2 g Fibre; 3 g Protein; 276 mg Sodium

Pictured on page 107.

Bean Sprout Chop Suey

If you like bean sprouts, you'll love this dish!
The perfectly cooked vegetables are coated in a tasty sauce.

Condensed chicken broth (see Note)	1/4 cup	60 mL
Cornstarch	1 1/2 tbsp.	25 mL
Soy sauce	2 tbsp.	30 mL
Rice vinegar	2 tsp.	10 mL
Sesame oil (optional)	1 tsp.	5 mL
Granulated sugar	1 tsp.	5 mL
Ground ginger	1/2 tsp.	2 mL
Cooking oil	1 tbsp.	15 mL
Medium onion, halved lengthwise and sliced	1	1
Celery rib, thinly sliced	1	1
Finely shredded cabbage	1 cup	250 mL
Garlic cloves, minced (or 1/2 tsp., 2 mL, powder)	2	2
Fresh bean sprouts, cut once if desired	5 cups	1.25 L
Green onion, thinly sliced	1	1

Stir broth into cornstarch in small dish. Add next 5 ingredients. Stir. Set aside.

Heat wok or large frying pan on medium-high until very hot. Add cooking oil. Add onion, celery, cabbage and garlic. Stir-fry for about 2 minutes until starting to brown and soften.

Add bean sprouts. Stir-fry for about 1 minute until heated through. Stir broth mixture. Stir into cabbage mixture on medium for 1 to 2 minutes until boiling and thickened.

Sprinkle with green onion just before serving. Makes 5 cups (1.25 L). Serves 4.

1 serving: 103 Calories; 3.9 g Total Fat (2.2 g Mono, 1.2 g Poly, 0.4 g Sat); trace Cholesterol; 14 g Carbohydrate; 2 g Fibre; 5 g Protein; 646 mg Sodium

Note: If you prefer not to open a 10 oz. (284 mL) can of condensed chicken broth (to only use 1/4 cup, 60 mL), make a double strength chicken broth using 1/4 cup (60 mL) hot water and 1 tsp. (5 mL) chicken bouillon powder. The taste will be slightly different.

Vegetable Dishes

Braised Vegetables

Fresh bok choy and crunchy water chestnuts combine with a caramel-coloured sauce in this tasty, mildly spicy dish. Adjust the amount of chili paste to suit your tastes.

Water	1 tbsp.	15 mL
Cornstarch	2 tsp.	10 mL
Chinese dried mushrooms	6	6
Boiling water, to cover		
Peanut (or cooking) oil	1 tbsp.	15 mL
Heads of Shanghai bok choy	3	3
Heads of baby bok choy	2	2
Can of sliced water chestnuts, drained	8 oz.	227 mL
Green onions, cut into 1 inch (2.5 cm) pieces	8	8
Prepared vegetable broth	1/4 cup	60 mL
Low-sodium soy sauce	1 tbsp.	15 mL
Hoisin sauce	1 tbsp.	15 mL
Chili paste (sambal oelek)	1 tsp.	5 mL

Stir water into cornstarch in small cup. Set aside.

Put mushrooms into small bowl. Add boiling water. Let stand for 20 minutes until softened. Drain. Remove and discard stems. Slice caps thinly.

Heat wok or large frying pan on medium-high until very hot. Add peanut oil. Add mushrooms and next 4 ingredients. Stir-fry for 1 minute.

Combine broth, soy sauce, hoisin sauce and chili paste in separate small bowl. Add to vegetable mixture. Stir-fry for about 3 minutes until vegetables are tender-crisp. Stir cornstarch mixture. Stir into vegetable mixture until vegetables are coated and sauce is thickened. Do not overcook. Makes 8 cups (2 L).

1 cup (250 mL): 60 Calories; 1.9 g Total Fat (0.8 g Mono, 0.6 g Poly, 0.3 g Sat); 0 mg Cholesterol; 10 g Carbohydrate; 1 g Fibre; 2 g Protein; 226 mg Sodium

Pictured on page 126.

Suey Choy With Honey

This tangy vegetable dish has a hint of sweetness and a mild citrus flavour.

Orange juice	1/4 cup	60 mL
Cornstarch	2 tsp.	10 mL
Liquid honey	1 tbsp.	15 mL
Dry sherry	2 tsp.	10 mL
Soy sauce	1 tsp.	5 mL
Sesame oil	1 tsp.	5 mL
Sesame seeds, toasted (see Tip, page 103)	1 tsp.	5 mL
Cooking oil	1 tbsp.	15 mL
Sliced celery	1/2 cup	125 mL
Thinly sliced carrot	1/4 cup	60 mL
Garlic cloves, minced (or 1/4 – 1/2 tsp., 1 – 2 mL, powder)	1 – 2	1 – 2
Finely grated peeled gingerroot	1 tsp.	5 mL
Suey choy (Chinese cabbage) leaves, shredded (about 1 lb., 454 g)	22	22
Green onions, sliced	2	2

Stir orange juice into cornstarch in small bowl. Add next 5 ingredients. Stir. Set aside.

Heat wok or large frying pan on medium-high until very hot. Add cooking oil. Add celery, carrot, garlic and ginger. Stir-fry for 30 seconds. Add suey choy and green onion. Stir-fry for 1 minute. Stir cornstarch mixture. Stir into suey choy mixture for about 1 minute until boiling and thickened. Makes 3 cups (750 mL). Serves 4.

1 serving: 106 Calories; 5.3 g Total Fat (2.7 g Mono, 1.8 g Poly, 0.5 g Sat); 0 mg Cholesterol; 14 g Carbohydrate; 2 g Fibre; 2 g Protein; 120 mg Sodium

Pictured on page 108.

Paré Pointer

Wokking a fine line.

Two-Colour Vegetables

Bright green broccoli and tender-crisp cauliflower are coated in a very pleasant sauce. The light sprinkling of sesame seeds adds a delicate nutty flavour.

Prepared chicken broth	3/4 cup	175 mL
Cornstarch	2 tsp.	10 mL
Soy sauce	2 tsp.	10 mL
Granulated sugar	1/2 tsp.	2 mL
Sesame oil (optional)	1/2 tsp.	2 mL
Garlic powder	1/8 tsp.	0.5 mL
Cooking oil	2 tsp.	10 mL
Cauliflower florets	3 cups	750 mL
Prepared chicken broth	2 tbsp.	30 mL
Cooking oil	2 tsp.	10 mL
Broccoli florets	3 cups	750 mL
Prepared chicken broth	2 tbsp.	30 mL
Sesame seeds, toasted (see Tip, page 103)	1 tsp.	5 mL

Stir first amount of broth into cornstarch in small bowl. Add next 4 ingredients. Stir. Set aside.

Heat wok or large frying pan on medium-high until very hot. Add first amount of cooking oil. Add cauliflower. Stir-fry for 1 minute. Add second amount of broth. Cover. Cook for about 2 minutes until tender-crisp. Turn out onto 1 side of serving plate. Cover.

Heat second amount of cooking oil in wok on medium-high. Add broccoli. Stir-fry for 30 seconds. Add third amount of broth. Cover. Cook for about 1 minute until bright green and tender-crisp. Turn out beside cauliflower on serving plate. Cover. Stir cornstarch mixture. Add to wok. Heat and stir on medium-high until boiling. Cook for about 5 minutes until reduced and slightly thickened. Pour over vegetables.

Sprinkle with sesame seeds. Makes about 4 1/2 cups (1.1 L). Serves 4.

1 serving: 104 Calories; 5.8 g Total Fat (3 g Mono, 1.8 g Poly, 0.6 g Sat); 0 mg Cholesterol; 10 g Carbohydrate; 3 g Fibre; 5 g Protein; 420 mg Sodium

Pictured on page 89.

Asparagus In Sizzling Sauce

These glistening greens have a nutty, slightly salty flavour.

Fresh asparagus, trimmed of tough ends and cut into 3/4 inch (2 cm) pieces (about 3 cups, 750 mL)	1 lb.	454 g
Boiling water	6 cups	1.5 L
Peanut (or cooking) oil	2 tbsp.	30 mL
Oyster sauce	2 tbsp.	30 mL
Sesame oil	1 tsp.	5 mL

Cook asparagus in boiling water in large uncovered saucepan on high for 2 minutes. Drain. Place in hot cast-iron pan (as is traditionally done for "sizzling" dishes) or heated serving dish.

While asparagus is cooking, heat peanut oil in small saucepan on high until just starting to smoke. Immediately pour hot peanut oil over drained asparagus in hot pan. The peanut oil should sizzle when it hits the asparagus.

Add oyster sauce and sesame oil. Toss until coated. Makes 2 1/2 cups (625 mL). Serves 4.

1 serving: 96 Calories; 8.2 g Total Fat (3.7 g Mono, 2.7 g Poly, 1.4 g Sat); trace Cholesterol; 5 g Carbohydrate; 1 g Fibre; 2 g Protein; 743 mg Sodium

Pictured on page 144.

Paré Pointer
Wok me up and throw away the ghee.

Chinese Stir-Fry Vegetables

This wholesome, healthy dish is so easy to make! Fresh garden vegetables are tossed in a sauce that won't overpower your taste buds.

Prepared chicken broth	1/2 cup	125 mL
Cornstarch	1 tbsp.	15 mL
Soy sauce	2 tsp.	10 mL
Granulated sugar	1 1/2 tsp.	7 mL
Salt	1 tsp.	5 mL
Cooking oil	2 tbsp.	30 mL
Small cauliflower florets	3/4 cup	175 mL
Small broccoli florets	3/4 cup	175 mL
Thinly sliced carrot	3/4 cup	175 mL
Thinly sliced celery	1/3 cup	75 mL
Fresh pea pods	2 1/4 cups	550 mL
Sliced fresh white mushrooms	1 1/2 cups	375 mL
Thinly sliced green onion	1/3 cup	75 mL

Stir broth into cornstarch in small bowl. Add soy sauce, sugar and salt. Stir. Set aside.

Heat wok or large frying pan on medium-high until very hot. Add cooking oil. Add remaining 7 ingredients. Stir-fry for 3 to 5 minutes until tender-crisp. Stir broth mixture. Stir into vegetable mixture for about 2 minutes until boiling and thickened. Makes 5 cups (1.25 L). Serves 4.

1 serving: 144 Calories; 7.5 g Total Fat (4.2 g Mono, 2.3 g Poly, 0.6 g Sat); 0 mg Cholesterol; 16 g Carbohydrate; 3 g Fibre; 5 g Protein; 915 mg Sodium

Pictured on page 90.

 The fresh gingerroot found in your local grocery stores has a thick, bitter-tasting skin that needs to be peeled before using.

Bean Sprout Salad

*A light, refreshing mix of bean sprouts, cucumber
and green onion. The ginger and soy sauce add a touch
of flavour to this otherwise mild salad.*

Water	8 cups	2 L
Fresh bean sprouts	1 1/2 lbs.	680 g
English cucumber (with peel), cut into 2 inch (5 cm) matchsticks	1 cup	250 mL
Sliced green onion	1 cup	250 mL
White vinegar	2 tbsp.	30 mL
Sesame oil	1 tbsp.	15 mL
Granulated sugar	1 tbsp.	15 mL
Soy sauce	1 tbsp.	15 mL
Salt	1/2 tsp.	2 mL
Finely grated peeled gingerroot	1/4 tsp.	1 mL
Chili paste (sambal oelek), optional	1/4 tsp.	1 mL

Bring water to a boil in medium saucepan on medium-high. Add bean sprouts. Turn off heat. Let stand for 1 minute. Drain. Rinse with cold water. Drain well. Turn into serving dish.

Add cucumber and green onion. Toss.

Combine remaining 7 ingredients in small bowl. Add to cucumber mixture. Toss. Chill. Makes 6 1/2 cups (1.6 L). Serves 8.

1 serving: 55 Calories; 1.9 g Total Fat (0.7 g Mono, 0.8 g Poly, 0.3 g Sat); 0 mg Cholesterol; 8 g Carbohydrate; 1 g Fibre; 3 g Protein; 286 mg Sodium

 For a prettier presentation, pinch off both ends of bean sprouts before adding to the recipe.

Banana Fritters

These soft, deep-fried bananas are drizzled with a sweet, rich caramel sauce. Serve with ice cream to make this mouth-watering dessert even more delectable.

All-purpose flour	1 cup	250 mL
Baking powder	2 tsp.	10 mL
Baking soda	1/4 tsp.	1 mL
Water	1 1/4 cups	300 mL
Medium bananas, cut into 3 inch (7.5 cm) pieces	4	4
All-purpose flour	2 tbsp.	30 mL
Cooking oil, for deep-frying		
CARAMEL SAUCE		
Hard margarine (or butter)	1/3 cup	75 mL
Brown sugar, packed	1 cup	250 mL
Water	1/3 cup	75 mL
Cornstarch	1 tbsp.	15 mL
Whipping cream	1/2 cup	125 mL

Combine first 3 ingredients in large bowl. Make a well in centre.

Add water to well. Stir until batter is smooth.

Coat banana in second amount of flour. Dip into batter.

Deep-fry, in 2 to 3 batches, in hot (350°F, 175°C) cooking oil for 3 to 5 minutes until golden brown. Remove to paper towels to drain.

Caramel Sauce: Combine all 5 ingredients in medium saucepan. Heat and stir on medium-high for 5 to 10 minutes until boiling and thickened. Makes 1 1/2 cups (375 mL) sauce. Drizzle over banana. Serves 4.

1 serving: 767 Calories; 34 g Total Fat (17.6 g Mono, 4.2 g Poly, 10.4 g Sat); 37 mg Cholesterol; 115 g Carbohydrate; 3 g Fibre; 6 g Protein; 489 mg Sodium

Pictured on page 143.

Sweet Fried Walnuts

These brown, sugared walnuts have a toasted flavour and go well with green tea. Enjoy them as a light dessert or as a snack.

Walnut halves	**2 cups**	**500 mL**
Boiling water, to cover		
Granulated sugar	**1/2 cup**	**125 mL**
Cooking oil, for deep-frying		

Add walnuts to boiling water in medium saucepan. Bring to a boil. Boil for 1 minute. Drain well.

Add sugar. Toss until coated. Spread on baking sheet. Let stand overnight to dry.

Deep-fry, in 2 batches, in hot (375°F, 190°C) cooking oil for about 1 1/2 minutes until golden brown. Remove to baking sheet. Cool. Blot with paper towel. Makes 2 cups (500 mL).

1/4 cup (60 mL): 267 Calories; 21.5 g Total Fat (6.8 g Mono, 11.9 g Poly, 1.8 g Sat); 0 mg Cholesterol; 18 g Carbohydrate; 1 g Fibre; 4 g Protein; 3 mg Sodium

Pictured on page 143.

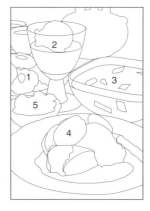

1. Almond Cookies, page 145
2. Lychees And Mandarin Ice, page 149
3. Almond Fruit Soup, page 148
4. Banana Fritters, page 141
5. Sweet Fried Walnuts, above

Props Courtesy Of: Casa Bugatti
Danesco Inc.
Kitchen Treasures
Pier 1 Imports
The Bay

Almond Cookies

*These melt-in-your-mouth cookies are attractive
and they taste great! Using skinned almonds is more
traditional, but they also look very pretty with the skin.*

Hard margarine (or butter), softened	1 cup	250 mL
Granulated sugar	1 cup	250 mL
Large egg	1	1
Almond flavouring	1 1/2 tsp.	7 mL
All-purpose flour	3 cups	750 mL
Baking soda	1 tsp.	5 mL
Salt	1/2 tsp.	2 mL
Whole almonds (with or without skin)	80	80

Cream margarine and sugar in large bowl. Beat in egg and almond flavouring until light and fluffy.

Add flour, baking soda and salt. Mix well. Shape into 1 inch (2.5 cm) balls. Arrange on ungreased cookie sheet. Press with bottom of glass to flatten.

Press 1 almond into centre of each cookie. Bake in 350°F (175°C) oven for about 12 minutes until edges are golden. Makes 80 cookies.

1 cookie: 57 Calories; 3.1 g Total Fat (1.9 g Mono, 0.4 g Poly, 0.6 g Sat); 3 mg Cholesterol; 7 g Carbohydrate; trace Fibre; 1 g Protein; 60 mg Sodium

Pictured on page 143.

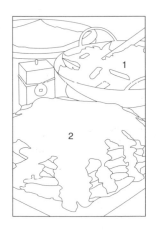

1. Asparagus In Sizzling Sauce, page 138
2. Shrimp Omelet Stack, page 98

Props Courtesy Of: Canhome Global
Danesco Inc.

Fortune Cookies

These are so much fun to serve your guests. They are crisp and sweet with a pleasing vanilla flavour. Don't forget to include your own unique fortunes!

All-purpose flour	1/2 cup	125 mL
Cornstarch	1 tbsp.	15 mL
Granulated sugar	1/4 cup	60 mL
Salt	1/4 tsp.	1 mL
Egg white (large)	1	1
Hard margarine (or butter), melted	1/4 cup	60 mL
Water	2 tbsp.	30 mL
Vanilla	1 tsp.	5 mL

Fortunes typed on narrow paper strips,
   about 3 inches (7.5 cm) long

Stir flour, cornstarch, sugar and salt in small bowl. Make a well in centre.

Add egg white, margarine, water and vanilla to well. Stir with whisk until smooth. Spread scant 1 tbsp. (15 mL) batter on greased cookie sheet into 3 1/2 inch (9 cm) circle. Repeat, making 2 cookies at a time. Bake on centre rack in 300°F (150°C) oven for 10 to 11 minutes until starting to turn golden around edge.

Working quickly as cookie hardens as it cools, remove 1 cookie from cookie sheet with spatula onto tea towel. 1. Bring 2 opposite edges together over centre using tea towel to protect hands from heat. Insert fortune into cookie. 2. Lift cookie from tea towel and "drape" over edge of glass, pulling ends down to make crease at centre of cookie. Place upright in muffin pan to hold shape while cooling. Repeat with second cookie. Re-warm in oven if necessary to form more easily. Repeat with remaining batter, 2 cookies at a time, greasing cookie sheet each time. It is best to use cooled cookie sheet each time so using 2 cookie sheets works well and also goes much faster. Makes about 18 cookies.

1 cookie: 52 Calories; 2.7 g Total Fat (1.8 g Mono, 0.3 g Poly, 0.6 g Sat); 0 mg Cholesterol; 6 g Carbohydrate; trace Fibre; 1 g Protein; 68 mg Sodium

Pictured on front cover.

(continued on next page)

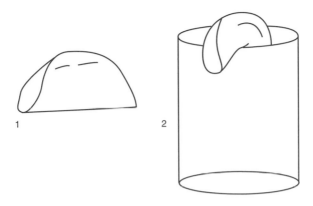

1   2

 To include a fortune, type a variety of sayings onto a piece of paper. Cut paper into strips, with one fortune per strip. Use the suggestions below, Paré Pointers or make up your own.

You will enjoy good health and a long life.

You will be successful in love.

You will get exactly what you deserve.

You will have a happy home and many friends.

You have a creative mind.

Believe in your dreams.

You will be surrounded by warmth and luxury.

Make a wish.

You like to make new friends.

Your business will be profitable.

You have a magnetic personality.

Good news will come your way.

Almond Fruit Soup

A fresh, light dessert that would make the perfect finish to your Chinese meal. This is so easy to make! Serve cold.

Envelope of unflavoured gelatin	1/4 oz.	7 g
Cold water	1/4 cup	60 mL
Skim evaporated milk	1 1/3 cups	325 mL
Granulated sugar	1 tbsp.	15 mL
Almond flavouring	1 tsp.	5 mL
Water	3/4 cup	175 mL
Granulated sugar	1/4 cup	60 mL
Can of fruit cocktail (with syrup), chilled	14 oz.	398 mL

Sprinkle gelatin over cold water in small saucepan. Let stand for 1 minute.

Add evaporated milk and first amount of sugar. Heat and stir on medium until gelatin and sugar are dissolved. Remove from heat.

Stir in almond flavouring. Pour into lightly greased 8 × 8 inch (20 × 20 cm) pan. Chill for several hours until firm. Cut lines diagonally through gelatin 1/2 inch (12 mm) apart. Cut straight lines 1/2 inch (12 mm) apart, forming small diamond shapes. Loosen diamonds from pan using straight-edged pancake lifter. Turn into decorative serving bowl.

Combine water and second amount of sugar in small saucepan. Bring to a boil. Boil for 2 minutes. Cool slightly. Chill. Pour over gelatin in serving bowl. Stir gently.

Add fruit cocktail with syrup. Stir. Makes 3 1/2 cups (875 mL). Serves 6.

1 serving: 133 Calories; 0.2 g Total Fat (0.1 g Mono, trace Poly, 0.1 g Sat); 2 mg Cholesterol; 28 g Carbohydrate; 1 g Fibre; 6 g Protein; 76 mg Sodium

Pictured on page 143.

Lychees And Mandarin Ice

Sweet lychee fruit is topped with an icy mandarin sorbet.
Serve in an elegant glass for a cool, refreshing treat.

Water	1 cup	250 mL
Granulated sugar	1 cup	250 mL
Finely grated peeled gingerroot	1 tsp.	5 mL
Can of mandarin orange segments (with juice)	10 oz.	284 mL
Orange-flavoured liqueur (such as Grand Marnier)	2 tbsp.	30 mL
Can of lychee fruit (with syrup), chilled	20 oz.	565 mL

Combine first 3 ingredients in medium saucepan. Heat and stir on medium-low until sugar is dissolved. Bring to a boil on medium-high. Boil, uncovered, without stirring, for about 10 minutes until mixture is slightly thickened. Cool until lukewarm.

Process orange segments with juice in blender until smooth. Add to sugar mixture.

Add liqueur. Stir. Pour into 9 x 9 inch (22 x 22 cm) pan. Freeze for at least 6 hours or overnight, stirring occasionally, until set.

Divide and spoon lychee and syrup among 4 serving glasses. Scoop mandarin mixture over lychee. Serve immediately. Serves 4.

1 serving: 339 Calories; 0.5 g Total Fat (trace Mono, trace Poly, 0 g Sat); 0 mg Cholesterol; 82 g Carbohydrate; 1 g Fibre; 1 g Protein; 6 mg Sodium

Pictured on page 143.

Paré Pointer
If you're going to talk the talk, you need to wok the wok.

Measurement Tables

Throughout this book measurements are given in Conventional and Metric measure. To compensate for differences between the two measurements due to rounding, a full metric measure is not always used. The cup used is the standard 8 fluid ounce. Temperature is given in degrees Fahrenheit and Celsius. Baking pan measurements are in inches and centimetres as well as quarts and litres. An exact metric conversion is given below as well as the working equivalent (Metric Standard Measure).

Spoons

Conventional Measure	Metric Exact Conversion Millilitre (mL)	Metric Standard Measure Millilitre (mL)
$1/8$ teaspoon (tsp.)	0.6 mL	0.5 mL
$1/4$ teaspoon (tsp.)	1.2 mL	1 mL
$1/2$ teaspoon (tsp.)	2.4 mL	2 mL
1 teaspoon (tsp.)	4.7 mL	5 mL
2 teaspoons (tsp.)	9.4 mL	10 mL
1 tablespoon (tbsp.)	14.2 mL	15 mL

Cups

Conventional Measure	Metric Exact Conversion Millilitre (mL)	Metric Standard Measure Millilitre (mL)
$1/4$ cup (4 tbsp.)	56.8 mL	60 mL
$1/3$ cup ($5^1/3$ tbsp.)	75.6 mL	75 mL
$1/2$ cup (8 tbsp.)	113.7 mL	125 mL
$2/3$ cup ($10^2/3$ tbsp.)	151.2 mL	150 mL
$3/4$ cup (12 tbsp.)	170.5 mL	175 mL
1 cup (16 tbsp.)	227.3 mL	250 mL
$4^1/2$ cups	1022.9 mL	1000 mL (1 L)

Dry Measurements

Conventional Measure Ounces (oz.)	Metric Exact Conversion Grams (g)	Metric Standard Measure Grams (g)
1 oz.	28.3 g	28 g
2 oz.	56.7 g	57 g
3 oz.	85.0 g	85 g
4 oz.	113.4 g	125 g
5 oz.	141.7 g	140 g
6 oz.	170.1 g	170 g
7 oz.	198.4 g	200 g
8 oz.	226.8 g	250 g
16 oz.	453.6 g	500 g
32 oz.	907.2 g	1000 g (1 kg)

Oven Temperatures

Fahrenheit (°F)	Celsius (°C)
175°	80°
200°	95°
225°	110°
250°	120°
275°	140°
300°	150°
325°	160°
350°	175°
375°	190°
400°	205°
425°	220°
450°	230°
475°	240°
500°	260°

Pans

Conventional Inches	Metric Centimetres
8x8 inch	20x20 cm
9x9 inch	22x22 cm
9x13 inch	22x33 cm
10x15 inch	25x38 cm
11x17 inch	28x43 cm
8x2 inch round	20x5 cm
9x2 inch round	22x5 cm
10x4$1/2$ inch tube	25x11 cm
8x4x3 inch loaf	20x10x7.5 cm
9x5x3 inch loaf	22x12.5x7.5 cm

Casseroles

CANADA & BRITAIN Standard Size Casserole	Exact Metric Measure	UNITED STATES Standard Size Casserole	Exact Metric Measure
1 qt. (5 cups)	1.13 L	1 qt. (4 cups)	900 mL
$1^1/2$ qts. ($7^1/2$ cups)	1.69 L	$1^1/2$ qts. (6 cups)	1.35 L
2 qts. (10 cups)	2.25 L	2 qts. (8 cups)	1.8 L
$2^1/2$ qts. ($12^1/2$ cups)	2.81 L	$2^1/2$ qts. (10 cups)	2.25 L
3 qts. (15 cups)	3.38 L	3 qts. (12 cups)	2.7 L
4 qts. (20 cups)	4.5 L	4 qts. (16 cups)	3.6 L
5 qts. (25 cups)	5.63 L	5 qts. (20 cups)	4.5 L

Tip Index

B

Bean sprouts – for prettier presentation .140

C

Cookies – to make fortunes 147

F

Fortunes in cookies 147

G

Gingerroot – to use 139

M

Meat – to slice easily 69

N

Nuts – to toast 103

P

Peeling gingerroot 139

R

Removing skin from tomatoes 45
Rice
    to handle 131
    to use cold in recipe 131

S

Seeds – to toast 103
Slicing meat easily 69

T

Toasting nuts and seeds 103
Tomatoes – to remove skin 45

U

Using cold rice 131

Recipe Index

A

Almond Chicken. 70
Almond Cookies. 145
Almond Fruit Soup 148
Almonds, Diced Chicken And 68
Almonds, Salty Chinese 16
Appetizers
    Battered Dry Ribs 13
    Deep-Fried Wontons 14
    Egg Rolls 24
    Green Onion Cakes. 12
    Ham And Chicken Rolls 26
    Hot Mustard Sauce 27
    Plum Sauce. 23
    Princess Shrimp Rolls. 21
    Salty Chinese Almonds 16
    Sang Choy Bow 20
    Shrimp Crackers 25
    Shrimp Toast. 19
    Soy Dipping Sauce 27
    Sweet And Sour Sauce. 15
    Vegetarian Spring Rolls 22
Asparagus In Sizzling Sauce. 138

B

Baby Bok Choy In Hoisin. 133
Banana Fritters 141
Barbecue Sauce 106
Basic Dough. 39
Basic Pan-Fried Noodles 123
Battered Dry Ribs 13
Bean Sprout Chop Suey 134

151

Bean Sprout Salad 140
Beef
    Braised Beef Curry. 64
    Ginger 66
    Orange Beef And Broccoli 58
    Oyster Sauce. 59
    Sweet. 57
    Tender Beef And Cashews 62
Beef And Green Peppers 63
Beef And Mushrooms 65
Beef Broccoli 56
Beef Chop Suey 60
Beef In Black Bean Sauce 61
Beef Satay Noodles. 118
Bird's Nest Chicken. 84
Black Bean Sauce, Beef In 61
Black Bean Sauce, Seafood In 95
Black Pepper Chicken 85
Bok Choy In Hoisin, Baby 133
Braised Beef Curry 64
Braised Chicken And Noodles 83
Braised Vegetables 135
Broth, Vegetarian 46
Buns
    Cocktail 40
    Sweet. 41

C

Cantonese Chow Mein 122
Cantonese Har Gow 28
Caramel Sauce 141
Cashews, Chicken And 82
Cashews, Tender Beef And 62
Chicken
    Almond 70
    Bird's Nest 84
    Black Pepper. 85
    Braised Chicken And Noodles 83
    Coconut. 81
    Diced Chicken And Almonds 68
    Ham And Chicken Rolls 26
    Kung Pao 80
    Lemon 76

Moo Goo Gai Pan 78
Old Country 77
Oriental Noodle Soup 55
Pineapple 74
Satay 79
Sesame. 75
Chicken And Cashews 82
Chicken Chow Mein. 120
Chicken Foo Yong 73
Chicken Hot Pot. 86
Chicken Vegetable Soup 51
Chicken With Ginger 67
Chinese Pea Pods 132
Chinese Stir-Fry Vegetables 139
Chinese Tomato Soup. 45
Chinese Vegetable Rolls 30
Chop Suey
    Bean Sprout 134
    Beef 60
Chow Mein
    Cantonese 122
    Chicken 120
Cocktail Buns 40
Coconut Chicken 81
Coconut Custard Filling 43
Coconut Custard Tarts 43
Coconut Filling. 40
Cookies
    Almond 145
    Fortune. 146
Crab Foo Yong. 93
Crackers, Shrimp 25
Curry, Braised Beef 64
Curry Sauce, Shrimp In 104
Custard Filling, Coconut 43
Custard Tarts, Coconut 43

D

Deep-Fried Vegetarian Wontons 47
Deep-Fried Wontons. 14
Desserts
    Almond Cookies 145
    Almond Fruit Soup 148

152

Banana Fritters 141
Fortune Cookies 146
Lychees And Mandarin Ice. 149
Sweet Fried Walnuts 142
Diced Chicken And Almonds. 68
Diced Tofu And Noodles. 116
Dim Sum
   Basic Dough 39
   Cantonese Har Gow 28
   Chinese Vegetable Rolls. 30
   Cocktail Buns 40
   Coconut Custard Tarts. 43
   Pearl Balls. 37
   Sesame Seed Balls. 42
   Shrimp Tail Purses. 32
   Steamed Dim Sims 33
   Steamed Pork Dumplings 38
   Sweet Buns. 41
   Tofu And Shrimp Drops. 34
Dipping Sauce, Soy 27
Dough, Basic 39
Dry Ribs, Battered 13
Dumpling Hot Sauce 38
Dumplings
   Cantonese Har Gow 28
   Frying Pan Pork. 112
   Steamed Pork 38

E

Egg Flower Soup 52
Egg Foo Yong. 130
Egg Garnish. 51
Egg Rolls 24
Egg Wash. 40, 41

F

Fillings
   Coconut. 40
   Coconut Custard. 43
   Pork. 32
   Pork And Shrimp. 33
   Shrimp. 28

Fish & Seafood
   Cantonese Har Gow 28
   Crab Foo Yong 93
   Deep-Fried Wontons 14
   Egg Rolls 24
   Five-Spice Shrimp 87
   Garlic Shrimp And Broccoli 99
   Honey Sesame Shrimp. 103
   Lobster Foo Yong 102
   Mandarin Whole Fried Fish 96
   Pineapple Shrimp 94
   Princess Shrimp Rolls. 21
   Sang Choy Bow 20
   Satay Shrimp 88
   Seafood In A Potato Nest. 100
   Seafood In Black Bean Sauce 95
   Shrimp And Scallops 91
   Shrimp Ecstasy 97
   Shrimp Foo Yong 102
   Shrimp In Curry Sauce. 104
   Shrimp Omelet Stack 98
   Shrimp Tail Purses 32
   Shrimp Toast. 19
   Steamed Dim Sims 33
   Steamed Fish 105
   Tofu And Shrimp Drops. 34
   Wor Wonton Soup 48
   Yangtze Fried Rice. 128
Fish Ball Soup. 44
Fish Balls 44
Fish In Szechuan Sauce. 92
Five-Spice Ribs, Honey 106
Five-Spice Shrimp. 87
Foo Yong
   Chicken 73
   Crab. 93
   Egg 130
   Lobster. 102
   Shrimp. 102
Foo Yong Sauce 101
Fortune Cookies 146
Fried Crumbed Tofu 117
Fried Fish, Mandarin Whole 96
Fried Noodles, Basic Pan- 123
Fried Rice, see Rice

153

Fried Walnuts, Sweet 142
Fritters, Banana 141
Fruit Soup, Almond 148
Frying Pan Pork Dumplings. 112

G

Garlic Shrimp And Broccoli 99
Ginger Beef 66
Ginger, Chicken With 67
Green Onion Cakes 12
Green Peppers, Beef And 63

H

Ham And Chicken Rolls. 26
Ham Fried Rice. 129
Honey Five-Spice Ribs. 106
Honey Sesame Shrimp 103
Honey Wash. 40, 41
Hot And Sour Soup 49
Hot Mustard Sauce. 27
Hot Pot, Chicken 86
Hot Sauce, Dumpling 38

K

Kung Pao Chicken 80

L

Lamb, Mongolian. 115
Lemon Chicken 76
Lemon Sauce. 76
Lobster Foo Yong. 102
Lychee Pork. 113
Lychees And Mandarin Ice 149

M

Mandarin Ice, Lychees And 149
Mandarin Noodle Baskets 121
Mandarin Pancakes. 110

Mandarin Whole Fried Fish 96
Mongolian Lamb 115
Moo Goo Gai Pan 78
Moo Shu Pork And Pancakes. 110
Mushroom Fried Rice 127
Mushrooms, Beef And 65
Mustard Sauce, Hot 27

N

Noodles
    Basic Pan-Fried 123
    Beef Satay. 118
    Braised Chicken And 83
    Cantonese Chow Mein 122
    Chicken Chow Mein 120
    Diced Tofu And. 116
    Mandarin Noodle Baskets 121
    Oriental Noodle Soup 55
    Shanghai 124
    Vegetarian Spring Rolls 22
    Vegetarian Wonton Soup. 46

O

Old Country Chicken 77
Omelet Stack, Shrimp. 98
Onion Cakes, Green 12
Orange Beef And Broccoli. 58
Oriental Noodle Soup. 55
Oyster Sauce 30
Oyster Sauce Beef. 59

P

Pancakes, Mandarin 110
Pancakes, Moo Shu Pork And 110
Pan-Fried Noodles, Basic. 123
Pea Pods, Chinese 132
Pearl Balls 37
Pepper Chicken, Black 85
Peppers, Beef And Green 63
Pineapple Chicken 74

Pineapple Sauce 74, 94
Pineapple Shrimp 94
Plum Sauce 23
Pork
    Battered Dry Ribs 13
    Cantonese Chow Mein 122
    Deep-Fried Wontons 14
    Egg Rolls 24
    Frying Pan Pork Dumplings 112
    Ham And Chicken Rolls 26
    Ham Fried Rice 129
    Honey Five-Spice Ribs 106
    Hot And Sour Soup 49
    Lychee 113
    Moo Shu Pork And Pancakes 110
    Mushroom Fried Rice 127
    Oriental Noodle Soup 55
    Pearl Balls 37
    Sang Choy Bow 20
    Shrimp Tail Purses 32
    Steamed Dim Sims 33
    Steamed Pork Dumplings 38
    Sweet And Sour 109
    Sweet And Sour Ribs 114
    Wor Wonton Soup 48
    Yangtze Fried Rice 128
Pork And Shrimp Filling 33
Pork Filling 32
Pork Vegetable Soup 50
Potato Nest 119
Potato Nest, Seafood In A 100
Potato Nests, Small 119
Princess Shrimp Rolls 21

R

Ribs
    Battered Dry 13
    Honey Five-Spice 106
    Sweet And Sour 114
Rice
    Egg Foo Yong 130
    Ham Fried 129
    Mushroom Fried 127

Pearl Balls 37
    Steamed 131
    Yangtze Fried 128
Rolls
    Chinese Vegetable 30
    Egg 24
    Ham And Chicken 26
    Princess Shrimp 21
    Vegetarian Spring 22

S

Salad, Bean Sprout 140
Salty Chinese Almonds 16
Sang Choy Bow 20
Satay Chicken 79
Satay Noodles, Beef 118
Satay Shrimp 88
Sauces
    Barbecue 106
    Caramel 141
    Dumpling Hot 38
    Foo Yong 101
    Hot Mustard 27
    Lemon 76
    Oyster 30
    Pineapple 74, 94
    Plum 23
    Soy Dipping 27
    Sweet And Sour 15, 114
Scallops, see Fish & Seafood
Seafood, see Fish & Seafood
Seafood In A Potato Nest 100
Seafood In Black Bean Sauce 95
Sesame Chicken 75
Sesame Seed Balls 42
Sesame Shrimp, Honey 103
Shanghai Noodles 124
Shrimp, see Fish & Seafood
Shrimp And Scallops 91
Shrimp Crackers 25
Shrimp Ecstasy 97
Shrimp Filling 28
Shrimp Foo Yong 102

Shrimp In Curry Sauce 104
Shrimp Omelet Stack 98
Shrimp Tail Purses 32
Shrimp Toast 19
Small Potato Nests 119
Soups
   Chinese Tomato 45
   Egg Flower 52
   Egg Garnish 51
   Fish Ball 44
   Hot And Sour 49
   Oriental Noodle 55
   Pork Vegetable 50
   Vegetarian Wonton 46
   Wor Wonton 48
Soy Dipping Sauce 27
Spring Rolls, Vegetarian 22
Steamed Dim Sims 33
Steamed Fish 105
Steamed Pork Dumplings 38
Steamed Rice 131
Stir-Fry Vegetables, Chinese 139
Suey Choy With Honey 136
Sweet And Sour Pork 109
Sweet And Sour Ribs 114
Sweet And Sour Sauce 15, 114
Sweet Beef 57
Sweet Buns 41
Sweet Fried Walnuts 142
Szechuan Sauce, Fish In 92

T

Tarts, Coconut Custard 43
Tender Beef And Cashews 62
Tofu
   Diced Tofu And Noodles 116
   Fried Crumbed 117
Tofu And Shrimp Drops 34
Tomato Soup, Chinese 45
Translucent Wrappers 28
Two-Colour Vegetables 137

V

Vegetable Dishes
   Asparagus In Sizzling Sauce 138
   Baby Bok Choy In Hoisin 133
   Bean Sprout Chop Suey 134
   Bean Sprout Salad 140
   Braised Vegetables 135
   Chinese Pea Pods 132
   Chinese Stir-Fry Vegetables 139
   Suey Choy With Honey 136
   Two-Colour Vegetables 137
Vegetable Rolls, Chinese 30
Vegetable Soup, Chicken 51
Vegetable Soup, Pork 50
Vegetarian Broth 46
Vegetarian Spring Rolls 22
Vegetarian Wonton Soup 46
Vegetarian Wontons, Deep-Fried 47

W

Walnuts, Sweet Fried 142
Whole Fried Fish, Mandarin 96
Wonton Soup 48
Wonton Soups
   Vegetarian 46
   Wor 48
Wontons 46
Wontons
   Deep-Fried 14
   Deep-Fried Vegetarian 47
Wor Wonton Soup 48
Wrappers, Translucent 28

Y

Yangtze Fried Rice 128

Company's Coming cookbooks are available at retail locations throughout Canada!

EXCLUSIVE mail order offer on next page

Buy any 2 cookbooks—choose a 3rd FREE of equal or less value than the lowest price paid.

Original Series · CA$14.99 Canada · US$10.99 USA & International

CODE		CODE		CODE	
SQ	150 Delicious Squares	KC	Kids Cooking	FD	Fondues
CA	Casseroles	CT	Cooking For Two	CCBE	The Beef Book
MU	Muffins & More	BB	Breakfasts & Brunches	ASI	Asian Cooking
SA	Salads	SC	Slow Cooker Recipes	CB	The Cheese Book
AP	Appetizers	ODM	One-Dish Meals	RC	The Rookie Cook
DE	Desserts	ST	Starters	RHR	Rush-Hour Recipes
SS	Soups & Sandwiches	SF	Stir-Fry	SW	Sweet Cravings
CO	Cookies	MAM	Make-Ahead Meals	YRG	Year-Round Grilling
PA	Pasta	PB	The Potato Book	GG	Garden Greens
BA	Barbecues	CCLFC	Low-Fat Cooking	CHC	Chinese Cooking
LR	Light Recipes	CCLFP	Low-Fat Pasta	PK	The Pork Book ◀NEW▶
PR	Preserves	CFK	Cook For Kids		Sept 1/03
CH	Chicken, Etc.	SCH	Stews, Chilies & Chowders		

Greatest Hits Series

CA$12.99 Canada   US$9.99 USA & International

CODE	
ITAL	Italian
MEX	Mexican

Lifestyle Series

CODE	CA$16.99 Canada US$12.99 USA & International
GR	Grilling
DC	Diabetic Cooking

CODE	CA$19.99 Canada US$17.99 USA & International
HC	Heart-Friendly Cooking

Special Occasion Series

CODE	CA$19.99 Canada US$17.99 USA & International
GFK	Gifts from the Kitchen
CFS	Cooking for the Seasons

CODE	CA$22.99 Canada US$17.99 USA & International
WC	Weekend Cooking

CODE	CA$24.99 Canada US$19.99 USA & International
HFH	Home for the Holidays
DD	Decadent Desserts ◀NEW▶ Oct 1/03

Company's Coming
COOKBOOKS ®

COMPANY'S COMING PUBLISHING LIMITED
2311 – 96 Street
Edmonton, Alberta, Canada T6N 1G3
Tel: (780) 450-6223 Fax: (780) 450-1857
www.companyscoming.com

EXCLUSIVE Mail Order Offer

See previous page for list of cookbooks

Buy 2 Get 1 FREE!

Buy any 2 cookbooks—choose a **3rd FREE** of equal or less value than the lowest price paid.

Quantity	Code	Title	Price Each	Price Total
			$	$
		DON'T FORGET		
		to indicate your		
		FREE BOOK(S).		
		(see exclusive mail order		
		offer above)		
		please print		

	TOTAL BOOKS (including FREE)	**TOTAL BOOKS PURCHASED:**	$

	International	Canada & USA
Plus Shipping & Handling (per destination)	$7.00 (one book)	$5.00 (1-3 books)
Additional Books (including FREE books)	$ ($2.00 each)	$ ($1.00 each)
Sub-Total	$	$
Canadian residents add G.S.T(7%)		$
TOTAL AMOUNT ENCLOSED	$	$

The Fine Print

- Orders outside Canada must be **PAID IN US FUNDS** by cheque or money order drawn on Canadian or US bank or by credit card.
- Make cheque or money order payable to: **COMPANY'S COMING PUBLISHING LIMITED**.
- Prices are expressed in Canadian dollars for Canada, US dollars for USA & International and are subject to change without prior notice.
- Orders are shipped surface mail. For courier rates, visit our web-site: **companyscoming.com** or contact us:
  Tel: (780) 450-6223 Fax: (780) 450-1857.
- Sorry, no C.O.D's.

Gift Giving

- Let us help you with your gift giving!
- We will send cookbooks directly to the recipients of your choice if you give us their names and addresses.
- Please specify the titles you wish to send to each person.
- If you would like to include your personal note or card, we will be pleased to enclose it with your gift order.

☐ MasterCard ☐ VISA

_____ Expiry date

Account # _____

Name of cardholder _____

Cardholder's signature _____

Shipping Address

Send the cookbooks listed above to:

Name: _____

Street: _____

City: _____ Prov./State: _____

Country: _____ Postal Code/Zip: _____

Tel: (___) _____

E-mail address: _____

☐ YES! Please send a catalogue

Complete your Original Series Collection!

- 150 Delicious Squares
- Casseroles
- Muffins & More
- Salads
- Appetizers
- Desserts
- Soups & Sandwiches
- Cookies
- Pasta
- Barbecues
- Light Recipes
- Preserves
- Chicken, Etc.
- Kids Cooking
- Cooking For Two
- Breakfasts & Brunches
- Slow Cooker Recipes
- One-Dish Meals
- Starters
- Stir-Fry
- Make-Ahead Meals
- The Potato Book
- Low-Fat Cooking
- Low-Fat Pasta
- Cook For Kids
- Stews, Chilies & Chowders
- Fondues
- The Beef Book
- Asian Cooking
- The Cheese Book
- The Rookie Cook
- Rush-Hour Recipes
- Sweet Cravings
- Year-Round Grilling
- Garden Greens
- Chinese Cooking
- The Pork Book **NEW** Sept 1/03

COLLECT ALL Company's Coming Series Cookbooks!

Greatest Hits Series
- Italian
- Mexican

Special Occasion Series
- Gifts from the Kitchen
- Cooking for the Seasons
- Home for the Holidays
- Weekend Cooking
- Decadent Desserts **NEW** Oct 1/03

Lifestyle Series
- Grilling
- Diabetic Cooking
- Heart-Friendly Cooking

Canada's most popular cookbooks!